Raising Tiny Humans Successfully:

A (Not so) Serious Guide to Parenting

Including an Introduction to SleepTalk® the "best kept" parental secret for over 50 years.

By

KERRE BURLEY

COPYRIGHT © 2025 KERRE BURLEY

ALL RIGHTS RESERVED.

No part of this book may be reproduced, stored in a retrieval system, or transmitted in any form. Reproduction by electronic, mechanical, photocopying, recording means, or otherwise without prior written permission from the publisher, Kerre Burley, is strictly forbidden.

DISCLAIMER

The information, techniques, and examples provided in this book including the SleepTalk Protocol are for educational purposes only and are intended to support parents and caregivers. While every effort has been made to verify the accuracy of the content, the author assumes no responsibility for any errors, inaccuracies, or omissions.

This book is not a substitute for professional medical, psychological, or therapeutic advice. If advice concerning medical or psychological matters is needed, the services of a qualified professional should be sought. The SleepTalk® process is a complementary approach and should not replace medical or therapeutic treatments prescribed by a professional.

The examples within this book are intended to illustrate concepts and are not a guarantee of specific results. Everyone's experience and outcomes will be influenced by their unique circumstances, their commitment, and consistency in applying the techniques and tips provided throughout the book. No express or implied guarantees of success are made, and results may vary.

ISBN: 978-1-7637395-0-5

Table of Contents

Introduction 1

Chapter 1: Relax, Parenting Doesn't Have to Be a Stress-fest. 4

Chapter 2: Fun, Play, Laughter 18

Chapter 3: Investing Time & Energy Into Your Parenting Skills. 25

Chapter 4: Emotional Intelligence Yours/Theirs. 32

Chapter 5: You're Already an Influencer. 46

Chapter 6: Is Your Parenting Style A Match? 52

Chapter 7: Discover The SleepTalk® Solution. 68

Chapter 8: Phase 1 - The Foundation Phase 77

Chapter 9: Master Effective Communication. 82

Chapter 10: Autonomy - The Parenting Pillar We Often Overlook. 96

Chapter 11: The Ever-changing Family Dynamic. 102

Chapter 12: Parenting In the Digital Era. 106

The Joys of Parenting. 114

Final Word From The Author. 117

Introduction

As parents, we all want to do the best for our children, but let's be real, it can be overwhelming trying to keep up with all the different stages of development and the latest parenting trends. **Social media, influencers, friends, family and even your wider community, will all have opinions on the best way to raise your tiny humans.**

But don't worry, I've got your back. The fact that you are reading this book is a huge step forward, a giant leap into unknown territory. When it comes to parenting, there are countless books, articles, and experts who will tell you the "right" way to do things.

But let's be real, many of us are just doing the best we can as each and every one of our amazing children will have their own unique impact in this world.

Throughout this book, my theme is to encourage you to trial, test and trust your instincts with what works and doesn't work. **Certainly, you will pick up a few tips and tricks, but real change comes from activity, trial and error.** I encourage you to (in the words of Bruce Lee)

> *"Absorb what is useful, discard what is not, and add what is essentially your own"*

But what if you are hanging on by your fingertips and your parental world is spinning out of control?

My real-world advice, **begin at Chapter 7, get started** on one of the most safe and effective tools parents can have, **the amazing**

SleepTalk® process. This simple and effective protocol **empowers you to initiate positive change in your tiny humans easily and effortlessly.**

The process has transformed the lives of thousands of families around the world for over five decades and it will for you too. So get started straight away.

In this world of instant gratification, it is also important for us **not to have unrealistic expectations as parents** and come to understand **there will never be a holy grail of parenting perfection,** yes I guarantee sometimes your wins will be many but your "fails" will be epic as well. However if you are **willing to invest in your children (and yourself,) you can establish solid bonds and connections that will last a lifetime.**

Without a doubt, there will be many, many touching and poignant times where the experiences that await you as a parent will take your breath away. You may not know it yet, **whether you have toddlers who need taming or rebellious teenagers who need strangling, "Parental Bliss," is a real thing** and it's never too late to learn how to experience this unconditionally.

As you begin this amazing journey. I highly recommend making use of our action items, at the end of each chapter. Use a highlighter to mark any nuggets you discover and hold yourself accountable by following through on your activities and steps.

Whilst you will want to push on, taking the time to complete the activities and ponder the questions that will enhance your parenting outcomes and insights. You will do OK.

If I can quote, Dr Justin Coulson,

Kerre Burley

"You don't have to be the best parent in the world but only the best parent in your child's world."

So, remember to give love, laugh lots and be the reason your tiny humans smile today.

Parenting is not for the weak,
It's a test of strength and grace,
But with every sleepless night,
Comes a smile on your face.

We'll stumble, we'll fall,
But we'll get back up again,
For the love of our children,
Will be our guiding light, till the end.

We'll learn to multitask,
Like never before,
And we'll do it all with a smile,
And an open heart and door.

So here's to the parents,
The warriors of love,
We'll do whatever it takes,
To guide our children above.

Anon

Chapter 1

Relax, Parenting Doesn't Have to Be a Stress-fest.

If you just want to do better, you're in the right place.

Imagine this, its midnight, and you've got a toddler who refuses to hit the hay or a teenager who's breaking curfew for the umpteenth time this week. On top of that, you've got an important sales presentation to prepare for your boss at 8 am tomorrow. You're stressed, tired, and on the verge of pulling your hair out. It's like a pressure cooker waiting to blow! Do you yell, do you scream, do you discipline? Nothing seems to be the solution.

This is probably just one of a million scenarios you encounter every day. So, let's start by talking about practical tips to handle those nail-biting moments with your children. Will these issues magically disappear overnight? Probably not. But with a fresh perspective and some new strategies, you can manage these challenges without losing your marbles. We may need to lose a few battles to ultimately gain our peace.

First off, let's clear the air about the word **"discipline"**. It's often misunderstood; its origin means to teach or educate.

So, instead of thinking of it as a rigid set of rules, consider approaching your children's meltdowns or your teenagers' indiscretions with humour and empathy when encountering these "**teachable moments**". It will take some pressure off you, and you'll find that parenting can be a bit more enjoyable.

Relax, seriously!

Now, I get it, you might not consider yourself a "fat controller", a worrier or stress head, but learning to let go can be life changing. It's normal for parents to worry, stress about their children, but when it becomes overwhelming, it can take a toll on your well-being.

When you learn to ease up, you'll notice some significant changes in your physical and mental state and the home environment.

Excess worry can crank up your anxiety levels (and your children's), but when you start to chill out a bit, you'll feel calmer and emotionally steadier. Your mental well-being will thank you as you start to feel happier, more content, and at peace with your family life.

Your energy changes, you become more able to cope, you can think clearly. No need for mood stabilisers, you're less irritable, can create a more harmonious family atmosphere and tackle life's challenges with a clearer head.

Plus, your focus and productivity will skyrocket as well. I have had parents assure me that their relationships have improved once they eased off on their overprotective tendencies and begun trusting their own instincts.

I remember well, struggling in the first few weeks of homeschooling my last child, Sean - he was seven. I felt so capable at the start of each day but there was so much to do in a day, a rigid plan to follow and a timetable to keep. I knew I really had to succeed in doing this, as it was his future that was at stake.

Then Sean would walk into the room; some days he was perfect, we got the work done quickly, then other days he stretched me in so many ways, it would be 6pm and we still hadn't got past the morning's work. I wanted to yell and scream as we fell further and further behind as the weeks progressed. At the time, we were living overseas, so I had no support or back-up.

I felt I was failing as a parent, failing as his teacher and the stress and guilt was unbearable. I would get up on Friday and literally feel sick to the stomach. I would worry all weekend how we were going to catch up. I was exhausted and not overly pleasant to be around.

I was normally such a happy, positive mum, yet I had become almost obsessed with sticking to the timetable, no matter what. This was definitely not the most important thing in my life. I realised I had to get back to being the happy, bubbly, fun person and this became the most important priority for me.

We found solutions together - the school day was moved back two hours to a 10am start, Sean was allowed to sleep in, as I started doing Yoga in the morning and followed it with a Zumba class online. It wasn't long before Sean joined in, and while the Yoga was fun, the Zumba was hilarious, Sean spent most of the session "laughing his head off" on the couch at his "unco" (uncoordinated) mum.

The whole energy changed between us and amazingly, when we hit the classroom, we consistently got the academic work done faster, leaving more time in the afternoon for new fun adventures.

As I now work with a lot of home school parents, I do see many well-meaning parents going down this track. They stay cranky, stressed and obsessed for years and it is nice to turn this around.

Now I won't tell you, your children will stop pushing your buttons, as often I tell parents, that's their job and many are good at it. But we, as parents can get a little smarter and get ahead of the game.

If you have patterns of behaviour, major concerns and worries that are not serving you, you need to let them go.

You will notice your cortisol levels (those stress hormones) will start to decrease, restoring a healthier hormonal balance.

Your immune system will thank you too for dialling back the worry, making you less prone to illnesses and if you can get a little laughter into your day, your body will produce more feel-good hormones. You'll feel more energetic; your overall health will improve over time. It's not just about mental relaxation but also about taking better care of your body.

So, embrace the art of relaxation, let go of excessive worry. **Try seeing things from your child's eyes, more relaxed means more tolerant, empathetic and be able to cope with much more.**

Why you ask? Because parenting should be a little less stressful and a lot more enjoyable. So, **how do you get relaxed, stop yelling and go to your happy place?** One of the best pieces of advice I was given as a single mum of five boys was,

"Don't stress about anything out of your control."

Sounds so simple, doesn't it, but it worked. If I found myself starting to worry, I would check internally (particularly as my children got older), "Is there anything I can do about this?" If the answer was "no", I moved on, relaxed in the knowledge that there was absolutely nothing I could do about it.

Were there times I had to step up as a single mum? Most definitely but found yelling and screaming at the boys only put them into shutdown mode, achieving very little. It took a throat operation with over-strained vocal cords to learn my lesson.

I suddenly realised, I had to find another way to cope and communicate effectively with my headstrong tiny humans.

Now I am not saying it is easy, like many parents of today, I experienced sabotage and resistance from many others. I remember well, each and every time the boys returned from a visit to my ex or the ex-mother-in-law.

Experiencing three oppositional, resistant and antagonistic little nightmares, refusing and resisting me at every opportunity for weeks sometimes months before they would settle down.

(I remember thinking, "What are they putting in the water?")

It took a while, but I found a way to be calm, loving and supportive, without going overboard. Now, we are going to talk about communication skills later in the book, but it was making the time to talk with my sons in a relaxed attitude and staying calm, patient and consistent that proved successful in these situations.

As my boys became older, I learnt to focus on their feelings and worked hard on being more empathetic in situations. Certainly, I knew I was not necessarily the easiest person to live with. I replaced my disciplined and harsh approach (which, in hindsight, was the way I was brought up) with more useful "teachable" conversations, exploring, explaining and empowering my tiny humans to open up, particularly as they became older. **Sure as a working parent, finding the time was hard, but the time investment was well worth the effort.**

I remember using a dialogue that switched roles with my children when they had done something concerning or an action needing a conscious parent to address immediately.

I would begin the conversation very calmly with, "**Well, if you were me** (the parent), **how do you think** (the unacceptable behaviour) **would make you feel?**" Then I would listen. When they answered, calmly I would ask, "**Well was that your intention?**"

Often it was not. I did have good boys, but I learnt that boys, particularly as they become teenagers, do not think things through or rationalise the consequences of their actions for themselves or others. Throw a few mates into the mix and you have "Buckley's".

So I would come to the conclusion of many of our discussions with, "**Well, is there a lesson or something to learn here, if you were me, what do you think, in this situation, we should do about it, to try and make sure it never happens again?**".

I was always amazed at some of the unique solutions and active self-discipline that they came up with. **They often were much tougher on themselves, and it made my job a little easier.** Come to think of it, many of these difficult (and embarrassing) experiences and conversations are some of my most treasured memories, as they were handled gracefully and with love.

Reap the rewards by changing your thinking, attitudes and habits if they are not serving you or your children.

Set aside a bit of time each day for yourself to do something that puts a smile on your face. Whether it's a good book, a leisurely stroll or getting your zen on in a yoga class, go for it.

It's like a little reset button for your parenting mojo. And let the children know it's okay for you to have your space and downtime. If they want to join in, sure thing, but only if you're up for it.

Now I will admit, it's a daily juggle raising those tiny humans and sometimes your own needs slip through the cracks. But here's the thing: taking care of you is not just a luxury, it's a necessity, and it shows your children that self-care is cool.

Making "me time" a top priority starts with penciling it into your day. Maybe it's 15-30 minutes to meditate, call a friend or just sit in the sun. **Often, we can lose our identity when children come along, so find stuff you really dig. It's different for everyone. You want activities that light up your life and give you a boost.**

And don't be thinking "me time" must be a budget-buster. Or that you have to head off to that spa for the weekend. Simple and wallet-friendly options work like a charm – nature walks or grooving to tunes. If your schedule's wild, try locking in that "me time" at the same time daily – make it a routine, set your alarm on your phone and enter it in your calendar.

All parents race against the clock, so think about time management tricks like prioritising or bundling chores. It's a doable feat and worth every ounce of effort.

The toughest part about "me time" is finding the time and energy to make it happen. That's when you must get a bit crafty. For instance, if you've got young tykes, try slotting your "me time" during nap time or after bedtime. If your crew's older, get them to chip in with the littler ones so you can have your moment.

I'll let you in on a little secret – my hour of power used to be an uninterrupted soak in the tub. **It took my boys months to realise that bugging me during this lone luxury hour wasn't the way to go.** But, boy, was it worth it. Even now, as they have grown into adults with tiny humans of their own, they're still tossing bath bombs my way as treasured gifts for birthdays and Mother's Day.

Setting boundaries and keeping them is a must for "me time." It's all about learning to say "no" to stuff that doesn't line up with your priorities. Plus, put yourself first when necessary. **And don't overdo it on things like social media or work – a limit keeps the balance.**

I used to meet up weekly with a friend for coffee, and ironically, we would spend 30 minutes whinging about no time to be active, until we made a pact together to go walking instead. (Of course, with our take-away coffees) We never looked back.

I also had another friend who had five children and religiously would hire a sitter and go sailing once a month. I remember asking her once, what did she love the most the sun, wind, salt air, or just being one with the great outdoors?

She literally wasted no time at all by replying no, it's the time away from the children that is the most rewarding. **The peace and quiet.**

Don't forget those longer "date nights" or "we time" as well, with your partner. **Bottom line: "me time" and "we time" are non-negotiable for parents.**

It's like being on a plane, putting your own oxygen mask on before helping others. **Your better parents, setting an example, and finding more happiness and balance in your life when you do.**

So, if you are a grinder, mark it on your calendar, or your phone, find your joy, and stand your ground. Remember, taking care of yourself is not selfish – it's a must-do to be the best you for your family. Plus, it builds your character and shows even your younger children how important it is to respect yourself and your personal time.

"Being a parent is an adventure, not a chore."

As a parenting consultant, in my experience, the most effective parents are those who have developed a parenting plan. It's ironic that couples often spend months or even years planning for their wedding day and similarly, I see expectant parents dedicate nine months to preparing the nursery for a baby's arrival, perhaps read a few parenting books, or attending a course or two, feeling or hoping they are prepared.

I find couples rarely discuss their long-term parenting philosophies, values, beliefs or wishes for their future. They seldom explore what kind of parents they want to be or will be, whether they're on the same page regarding important issues, or what they truly prioritise in raising a child. **This lack of discussion about fundamental values and beliefs seems like a significant oversight.**

However, I am here to let you know it is never too late. Let's talk about how to connect with your partner, significant others or even ex's to share open and honest conversation and dialogue about your expectations and your game plan for parenting.

- What was great about your own childhood & what was not so good?
- How do you want your family to operate, manage your time? Whose going to do what, can you plan a village?
- How are you going to enable clear and effective communication and guidelines together?
- What is your deepest wish for your child/children? What sort of adult do you want them to grow up to be?
- How are you going to overcome challenges? What is it truly important to you for you to pass on?

Being a parent is not about perfection, it's about progress!

(Small steps towards a big goal is always progress)

I am pleased to say, keep reading as we are providing you with the secret sauce in any relationship, and it's super crucial when you're raising your children together.

Think about also carving out some "we" time every now and then to discuss any areas that need a unified plan.

I've seen couples who are miles apart when it comes to raising their tiny humans causing major clashes in a relationship and, even worse, leave the children feeling like they're in the middle of this never-ending tug-of-war.

As your children get older a dedicated "family night" is also a great idea to add to the mix. Encourage it to become a "fun family tradition". Parents can decide whether their older children can invite friends or extras or not. Either way, it's a safe space for everyone to chat, be heard, and feel the love (device-free zone).

Now, if you're rolling solo without a partner, think about slotting some upstanding role models into your children's lives. Teachers, tutors, sports coaches, aunts, uncles, or your closest pals – they're all very important people who can be there for you and your children when you need a hand.

Now, I will apologise in advance to anyone who may feel I am being very gender biased here, as I know in this day and age, it is not politically correct to hold this old-fashioned view, but despite the gender arguments raging at the moment, this is my true belief and observations from my own experience.

As a single parent, I involved all my children in sport from an early age, nippers (or flippers), little athletics, T-ball, cricket, soccer, futsal, tennis, cross country running and swimming. They were very active, boisterous, loud and some would say out of control from an early age.

Yes, they flourished in these sporting arenas, learning lessons for life, but I truly believe the secret ingredient, which influenced them the most, where the male coaches, managers and other dads that they met.

I didn't leave it to chance, I purposely vetted (yes I said *vetted) their future coaches or tutors based on their character, demeanor and leadership qualities. *I thoroughly believe all our tiny humans need suitable role-models in their lives. Yet again as parents, we need to not leave it to chance, or social media to choose them for us.*

We also need to be ever super vigilant and aware of our childrens outside relationships at all times.

Action Steps

List one item you will implement this week and one to schedule for the next.

- What really brings you joy?
- I am going to change_____ and create a special space and activity for me.
- I am going to work on scheduling special "we time" with my partner and create a special family tradition that we will do consistently from now on.

Chapter 2

Fun, Play, Laughter

Laughter is the magical elixir for anyone, and it's the ultimate health boost and stress-reliever.

So, it's time to make room for more chuckles in your life. Whether you are parenting preschoolers or teenagers, a little laughter can go a long way.

It's no secret that some of us parents tend to take this "parenting gig" a tad too seriously at times. We can turn into bullies, know-it-alls and even our children's worst enemies. We forget that the positive energy from laughter can reduce stress and create a happy home.

After all, the best way to have happy children is to be a happy parent! The best way to be a happy parent is to stop sweating the small stuff.

Laughter - benefits for children

Laughter isn't just good for the grown-ups; it's a game-changer for children too. Check out what it can do for your little ones:

Stress reduction Laughter triggers the release of endorphins, those feel-good hormones, and helps lower stress hormones. Result? A more relaxed, less anxious child.

Boost immune system . Just 30 seconds of giggles can power up the immune system, increasing the production of antibodies and activating immune cells, helping children ward off illnesses. Laughing improved circulation, relaxes muscles, and even lower blood pressure.

Enhanced mood. Laughing is like a natural mood booster. It can lift your child's spirits, making them less prone to negative emotions. It's a healthy outlet to release pent-up emotions and frustrations.

Strengthened resilience. Children who find humour in challenging situations often become more resilient and better equipped to handle life's ups and downs

Boosted self-esteem Laughter often stems from a sense of accomplishment or feeling appreciated and included in social settings. This can elevate a child's self-esteem and confidence.

Social bonding. Laughter is a social activity that tightens the bonds between children, fostering better connections and camaraderie. It is a social cue that helps children understand appropriate behaviours, like sharing, understand social norms, reducing the risk of bullying and cultivating a sense of belonging.

Improved pain tolerance. Laughter revs up the body's production of natural painkillers, which might just help your children endure discomfort more easily.

Cognitive development. Playful laughter is linked to learning, creativity, and cognitive development. It boosts problem-solving skills and enhances brainpower, often accompanies imaginative and creative play, crucial for a child's cognitive and emotional growth. It promotes exploration and experimentation.

Communication skills. It's a form of non-verbal communication that allows children to connect with others and express their feelings without words.

Many years ago, I owned and operated highly successful aquatic centres called "Giggles Swim Schools," here in Australia.

I based our whole program and facilities on NLP and Laughter Yoga Principals and designed an accelerated learn-to-swim curriculum on these modalities. **We completely turned our team, our facility and our swimming sessions into a positive, fun experience for our families.**

After a few short months, the results were staggering, we proved that our clients from babies through to adults learnt and retained their aquatics skills much faster than normal. The progress was extraordinary with all negative behaviour dissipated in our safe environment.

Ultimately, we earned international acclaim for our remarkable rapid results, using these principles of learning through laughter and positive attitudes. **I believe parents can do the same.**

Play (yes, adults too!)

We know, life as a parent can be demanding. But here's the thing, playtime isn't just for the children; it's for parents too. Remember, studies have shown that incorporating play and laughter into your daily routine can improve your overall well-being, reduce stress, and enhance your relationship with your children.

You might find it hard to believe, but recent studies indicate that a surprising percentage of parents admit they don't enjoy playing with their children and would rather be doing something else. It's time to change that! (Please do not let that be you)

Incorporating play into your everyday life can be as simple as making a game out of daily tasks.

Fold laundry while racing your children to see who can fold the most items in five minutes or have a kitchen dance party while cooking dinner.

But what about those days when you're stuck inside due to bad weather, or your children are feeling down?

If COVID taught us anything it's how to have fun and be inventive quirky and interesting, so go online to get some ideas.

Invent a family tradition - Why not a Friday Fun Night? We can get you started if you're stuck with plenty of fun indoor activities suitable for children of all ages (even teenagers!)

Raising Tiny Humans Successfully

- Simon Says/Charades
- Survivor (indoors)
- The Floor is Lava
- I Spy/20 questions
- Imaginary World Trip
- Red Light, Green Light
- Indoor Treasure Hunt
- Balloon Volleyball
- Indoor Mini Golf
- Indoor Bowling
- Shadow Puppets
- Obstacle Course
- Balloon Tennis
- Truth or dare
- Pictionary
- Would you rather?
- Two truths and a lie
- Name that tune
- Obstacle course
- Puzzle race
- Movie night
- Board game night
- Build a blanket fort
- Paper airplane contest

So, parents, embrace the play, let your hair down, and have some fun! Incorporating laughter and play into your routine won't just make you feel better. it will also strengthen your relationship with your children and enhance their overall well-being. Remember, a sprinkle of play goes a long way in building strong bonds and nurturing emotional intelligence.

And don't fret about teenagers, it's never too late to have fun with your tiny humans. I had a blast with my teenage son while on holidays at a pinball museum, then spent quality time playing his favourites at a time zone.

Sure, I was hopeless at them, but the laughter over my inadequacies was priceless. Spending quality time with teenagers can be fleeting but invaluable. If I don't tell his peers, he still enjoys playing chess and watching anime with me.

Occasionally our tribe would have a Mexican or an Italian night and my tiny humans would oversee decorating the dining room, selecting the music, researching and organising the activities. It was a hoot. (Be careful not use to much chilli or garlic)

So listen to all your tiny humans passions and trends, try to keep an open mind and be there for them. It's well worth the effort to foster emotional intelligence and create memories together.

Action Steps.

Write down three joyous activities that you share with your children.

1.

2.

3.

Chapter 3

Investing Time & Energy Into Your Parenting Skills.

Raising tiny humans is no easy feat. Between the never-ending laundry, meal prep and playdates, it's no wonder that many parents feel like they're constantly running on empty. But what if we told you that there's a way to make things a little easier on yourself?

Let's do a little soul searching. When you were a little tiny human, how well did your parents do? Did you feel loved, safe and secure? I certainly grew up in a time when not only parents, but teachers, coaches and educators would smack, cane, strap, yell, force and punish, no questions asked. It was accepted in society. Thankfully those days are long gone for us in the western world as we've moved into a gentler way of parenting.

Parents have a lot more support and resources to curb those frustrations. So concepts and parenting tips (including this text) to help improve your attitude to parenting can share more positive solutions as they become the new norm.

Gratitude and meditation were life changers for me. However, as there is so much already out there in the main stream already on these skills, **I am going to cover time management and prioritisation,** positive habits that will make your life a little easier.

It's easy to get caught up in the daily grind, and before you know it, the day is over, and you haven't even had a chance to take a breath. **One of the best ways to take control of your time is by creating a schedule. Then, prioritise and batch your jobs.**

Some simple "Time stacking" ideas to consider

- Listen to podcasts or audiobooks when driving, exercising, or heading to work.
- Consider online grocery shopping or home deliveries to save time.
- Arrange appointments and plan to run errands on the same day.
- Where possible, enroll children in extracurricular activities on the same day.
- Carpool with other parents when convenient.
- Utilise apps and set appointment reminders to assist with your scheduling and planning.
- Dedicate a specific day for weekly menu planning, shopping, batch cooking, budgets, finances or checking statements.

- Arrange cleaning and laundry on specific days, with age-appropriate chores drawn up on a schedule for the children if appropriate.
- Organise quality time with your spouse and/or children around exercise or outdoor activities like bush walks or bike riding.

Are you being resourceful and utilising all the resources available to you?

I am often amazed how many parents want to wear the red cape and run themselves into the ground, when ultimately, they do have loving partners, grandparents, friends or even older children who are willing to share the load. There is no shame in asking for assistance.

Today, we have a host of free apps that can also be used to make life easier. i.e family and household management. apps.

It is amazing how much we do which is surplus and can be removed or adapted. Even the simple act of preparing a meal plan can free up an enormous amount of time for families. This doesn't have to be a rigid plan that you need to stick to down to the minute, but rather a loose guideline that helps you prioritise your tasks and responsibilities.

For example, you might want to schedule in some "me time" for yourself every day, or make sure that you're dedicating some specific time to your relationships with your partner and children. It may mean you get up 30 minutes earlier in the day to enjoy that peaceful bliss before the storm.

Once you've got a handle on your schedule, **it's time to start prioritising. This is where it can be helpful to take a step back and**

think about what's truly important to you. Are you spending your time and energy on things that truly matter, or are you getting bogged down in the small stuff? **Sometimes it can be helpful to make a list of your goals and priorities and then use that to guide your decision-making.**

Yes, you need to take time to make time.

Now that you've got a schedule and you are prioritising the important things, it's time to start call in the troops. Involve your significant others into this, seek their input. **Trying to connect with utilise their thoughts about your system, will creates a strong foundation of support.**

When decluttering, it's often helpful to sort items into four main categories: Keep, Donate, Sell or Bin. By categorising items into these four areas, you can streamline the decluttering process and make it more manageable. It helps you make decisions about what to keep and what to let go of, ultimately creating a more organised and simplified living space. So may I suggest you do the same with your time management during your days.

Consider these four different areas for your parenting scheduling:

Urgent and important. These are tasks that require immediate attention and are crucial to your goals or well-being. Focus on completing these first. Examples include attending to a child's medical emergency, dropping off and picking up children from school, handling a household emergency, and helping your child with homework or an assignment almost due.

Important but not urgent. These tasks contribute to your long-term goals and well-being but may not be time sensitive. Schedule time for them to avoid them becoming urgent. Examples include doing some regular exercise, setting aside time for family bonding activities, designating a time slot for grocery shopping and meal prep for the week, batch cooking or preparing meals for the family, cleaning and doing household chores, and scheduling a specific time to handle household finances, pay bills, and review the family budget.

Urgent but not important. These tasks are time-sensitive but don't directly contribute to your long-term goals. Evaluate whether you can delegate or minimise them. Examples include answering personal emails that can wait, dealing with minor school-related issues, returning a phone call from a friend, and checking social media.

Not urgent and not important. These are tasks that neither contribute to your long-term goals nor require immediate attention. Minimise or eliminate them to free up time for more important activities. Examples include scrolling through social media for extended periods, watching mindless TV shows, playing video games excessively, binging or planning a family vacation for next year and setting time aside for research and reservations.

I remember a working mother once telling me she had no time for the two girls 8yrs and 10yrs on the weekends, they were lazy and just lazed about.

On further questioning, she admitted to spending all Saturday cleaning the house (before the cleaner came on Monday,) because her girls would do nothing but lay around. She felt that it was necessary not to be judged as a dirty family by the cleaner. Then on the Sunday, she was just too exhausted to go anywhere and still angry at the girls for not contributing.

I asked, if the mother had discussed this with her children or even asked them to help and she had not.

In fact, on the first discussion as I suggested, the children shared with their mother, they were bored and would be eager to help with the housework, if it meant they could do something with their mum over the weekends.

Although I didn't tackle with this mum the silliness of cleaning up before the cleaner came, **both daughters began to do more around the house when mum asks.** When I last checked in, they still pitch in every Saturday morning helping to allow them all to go out to the shops on Saturday afternoons together.

When raising tiny humans, parenting has nothing to do with perfection. Perfection should never be the goal - not for us, not for our tiny humans.

Learning together to live in an imperfect world, loving each other despite or even because of our imperfections - this will allow our little, tiny humans to grow, that is your goal.

Action Steps

- Write up your goal, display it somewhere you will see and be reminded every day.
- Think with ink: write down all the things you do in a day; now only highlight the really important tasks.
- Now, prioritise them or even time stack them, i.e. could you listen to that podcast as you're walking the dog?
- Now put a smiling face next to them and write a note how could you make them fun.

Chapter 4

Emotional Intelligence Yours/Theirs.

Alright, let's take a leisurely stroll into the fascinating world of emotional intelligence. But first, let's kick back and chat about you.

- Do your children defy you at every opportunity?
- Do they embarrass you, every time you take them out?
- Do they ever listen?
- Do they have an uncanny knack for pushing your buttons?

Well, as I have said already, that's kinda their job, and they're usually pros at it. So, before we delve into understanding your child's emotions, let's start with a little introspection. Getting to know your feelings, attitudes, triggers and history is like unlocking the treasure chest of emotional intelligence. **It might sound a tad fancy, but trust me, it's like a magic key that can open doors to a whole new level of understanding, both for you and your child.**

Emotional intelligence has been making the rounds in personal and professional development circles over the last two decades. And believe it or not, it's a nifty tool for enhancing your parenting skills.

Now, I won't sugarcoat it; it's not always a walk in the park. But here's the golden nugget: being a terrific role model for your children is something each and everyone of us, can pull off.

After all, children are like little sponges, absorbing every bit of your behaviour and your responses. So, consider the impact your actions have on their budding emotional intelligence.

As their parent, you hold the reins to help your child develop their emotional intelligence. It's all about teaching them how to navigate the rollercoaster of emotions, **how to step into someone else's shoes and see the world from their perspective, and how to tackle life's puzzles and predicaments.**

Now, let's break it down into a few essential aspects:

- **Self-awareness and self-regulation.** It's like tuning into your own emotional radio station. You become aware of your feelings and learn how to manage them in a way that's as smooth as silk.
- **Empathy and social skills.** It's like the dance of emotions. You start recognising and connecting with other people's feelings and learn to waltz with them through the highs and lows of life.
- **Motivation.** Picture it, as setting emotional goals for yourself and your family. You're like the cheerleader, rallying the team to foster a warm and emotionally healthy environment.

So, what's the deal with all this emotional intelligence when it comes to parenting?

Well, as I have mentioned your children are watching you like hawks. They learn by example, soaking in your behaviour and your responses to the world.

If you want them to be emotional intelligence superheroes, you need to be the superhero. Remember, children often copy what they see, so make it worth their while.

Here's a little story to make it stick, imagine your child throws a tantrum in the grocery store.

A low EI response might involve getting angry and giving them the **"Please act your age!" speech, or threats ("You'll walk home") or smacks. The meltdown continues out of control.** It's like adding fuel to the fire, and trust me, I've seen it all too often. But here's the plot twist:

A high EI response would be like playing the empathy card. You could acknowledge the child's feelings by lowering your voice and saying softly,

"I can see that you're upset now, let's finish the shopping and we can have a chat when we get to the car".

This simple act of letting your child know you have heard them, understood them and will give them your undivided attention very soon, can lead some to a calm and productive conversation a few minutes later.

It's like taking the wind out of the sails of even the most headstrong, determined, and occasionally wild child.

Young children can have big emotions and great difficulty in articulating or even controlling them. (For neuro-diverse children, I have been reading recent research from a company called

Mendability that suggest quickly using a child favourite scent or even an ice pack can be ideal ways change a child's state and cut a meltdown off at the pass.)

As parents when we understand that, it is fundamentally easier to remain calm and address each situation as it arrives but remember to work towards trial and error to find solutions that work for your children.

It's OK to be a little irritated with your tiny humans.

In a recent article called The Generational Gap by Pham An, he stated that parents will always have trouble understanding how music, hair and fashion sense are acceptable and tolerable for their children.

He then goes on to say the same older people have, in truth, always been dissatisfied and dismayed by intergenerational conflict, sharing that **in 400 B.C. the great philosopher Socrates complained about the youth of his time, scolding them for having many bad habits, contempt for authority and disrespect for their elders.**

So, in hindsight, nothing much has changed.

Did you know children under seven years of age really DO NOT have the thinking patterns or abilities to do any of these skills listed below?

(There is also significant scientific data that suggests teenage boys going through adolescence loose significant abilities temporarily as well).

- Consideration or Questioning
- Doubt or Consequences of Actions
- Detailing or Organised thoughts.

So, is the child the problem or could it be our unrealistic expectations?

Now I am not saying there won't be meltdowns but starting early with your tiny humans does improve things dramatically as they grow up and develop better management skills and have a trusting bond with you.

Now, let's assess your own emotional intelligence. Take a moment to ponder these aspects:

- **Self-awareness.** Can you recognise and understand your emotions, including their triggers and their impact on your behaviour? Do you take responsibility for your mistakes, or do you blame others?
- **Empathy.** How often do you actively listen to your child's feelings and perspective when they're upset or in a difficult situation?
- **Emotion regulation.** Can you stay cool as a cucumber when dealing with your child's emotional outbursts or challenging behaviours?
- **Social skills.** Are you dependable, trustworthy and the friendly neighbour who encourages your child to express their feelings openly and guides them in resolving conflicts and building positive relationships with others?
- **Motivation.** Can you set and work toward positive emotional goals for yourself and your family, like creating an emotionally healthy environment?
- **Recognising emotions in others.** How often do you help your child identify and understand the emotions of others,

like friends, family members, or peers, to promote empathy and social awareness?

Now, let's switch gears to observing your children.

Understanding their emotional intelligence is like exploring a mysterious forest filled with unique creatures, each with its own quirks. Here are some ways parents can work on supporting their children's emotional intelligence:

Time and attention (No, your phone doesn't count)

All children, no matter what age, crave your time and attention, so put down your phone and devices, and make the time to be interactive and observe your children.

We have an epidemic now with many busy parents being addicted to their screens and their children feeling invisible.

To ace this emotional intelligence game, there's one crucial technique: **active listening**.

It's like being a detective, paying close attention to what your children have to say, and responding in a way that shows you truly understand and care about their feelings.

So, whether it's sitting in silence with your burley teenagers or having a chat about people or characters, you're opening a dialogue about what they're experiencing and remaining impartial and non-judgemental (not always that easy at first).

Observation Keep a watchful eye on your child's behaviour, emotions, and social interactions.

Take note of how they react in different situations and around different people. Look for signs of emotional awareness, empathy, and self-regulation.

Are you a parent that breaks promises and does not follow through with your children?

Observe your children being children, don't set unrealistic expectations; your tiny humans are and should be curious little explorers. Part of developing emotional intelligence is letting them learn through experiences, the good and the bad.

A Dad once shared with me that he had gotten into the habit of a weekly walk along the outskirts of a golf course with his young 4 year old daughter every Saturday morning before he went to work.

Then one morning, she was taking longer than expected and he got very cranky and yelled at her for dawdling. She started to cry. It was only then he noticed the ducks in the pond.

His daughter was mesmerised by the mother duck and her six ducklings taking a swim. In his haste he had not even seen them. He felt terrible, as he recognised this was a special moment for them both to share.

He stopped and apologised to her. They sat down and talked about the ducklings then dawdled home collected flowers. Work had to wait.

Sadly the term "invisible teenager" is becoming a reality!

Teenagers feel unseen or unheard by their parents who are preoccupied with other issues & fail to recognise the emotional complexities of adolescence or dismiss their teenagers' concerns as trivial. **A teenager's needs might go unnoticed or be minimised,**

leaving their self-worth and self-esteem in tatters, causing a lack of motivation or engagement or total disconnections with parents.

Engage in conversation Strike up open and judgment-free conversations with your child about their feelings and experiences.

Ask them about their emotions, what triggered them, and how they handled those emotions. Encourage them to express themselves freely and create a safe and supportive space for them to share.

Are they hungry, angry, lonely or tired (HALT)?

Listen actively When your child talks about their experiences, concerns, and emotions, be an active listener. Validate their feelings and let them know you understand and empathise with their point of view. This makes them feel heard and respected, nurturing their emotional awareness.

Ask open-ended questions Instead of asking yes-or-no questions, use open-ended questions that encourage your child to express their thoughts and feelings in more detail. This can foster self-reflection and effective communication.

Promote problem solving Encourage your child to find solutions to their emotional challenges. When they encounter tricky situations, ask questions like, "What can you do to make this situation better?" This helps them develop emotional problem-solving skills.

Model emotional intelligence Children learn by example. Demonstrate emotional intelligence in your own life. Show them how you handle your emotions, resolve conflicts, and empathise with others. Your actions can be a powerful model for them.

Teach emotional vocabulary Help your child expand their emotional vocabulary by teaching them to label their feelings. This empowers them to recognise and express their emotions more precisely.

You can use books, games, or everyday situations to discuss emotions and their meanings.

Support social interaction Encourage your child to take part in social activities and interact with peers. Social experiences can help them practice empathy, communication, and relationship-building, all of which are integral to emotional intelligence.

Remember, emotional intelligence is like a tree, with roots that grow deep and branches that reach high. Children develop at their own pace, so don't rush it. The key is to provide a nurturing and supportive environment where children feel comfortable exploring and expressing their emotions.

As a parent, your role is to be their guide (not always their friend) but your presence and support throughout this beautiful emotional intelligence journey.

Raising respectful children

Being a parent is not for the faint of heart. It's a wild and wonderful ride filled with laughter, tears, and everything in between. **And while raising little humans can be challenging, it's also one of the most rewarding things you'll ever do.** One of the most important things we can teach our children is respect. And while it may seem like an impossible task at times, there are plenty of positive training strategies you can use to help guide your little ones towards becoming respectful adults.

First and foremost, it's important to lead by example as we have already mentioned. Children learn more from what we do than what we say. So if you want your children to be respectful, make sure you're modelling that behaviour yourself. This means treating everyone with kindness and respect, even when it's hard. It also means setting boundaries and sticking to them. **When you set clear expectations and follow through with consequences, you're teaching your children that their actions have consequences.**

Using manners, saying "please and thank you" yourself often sets the benchmark for children.

This was often the work of our elderly grandparents, aunties and uncles many years ago, however if you are a grandparent-less family, and removed from the family nucleus, you can endeavour to befriend or invite mild-mannered mature mentors into your life.

Many modern families do not believe in sharing or discussing family values and responsibilities and I think this is a mistake. Let's just talk about "manners". I meet many parents who think that manners are old-fashioned and not necessary, however I can tell you, when I travel in the East, I love watching how the younger generation respect and treat their elders and strangers with kindness.

The western culture could really learn something from this. As a parent, simply saying "please and thank you" yourself often sets the benchmark for children to do the same.

Be a positive role model

As a parent, you're the primary role model. So, if you want your children to be polite, respectful, and kind, try not to unleash road rage or potty mouth when someone takes your parking spot.

You are their hero, so act the part.

Another important aspect of raising respectful children is teaching them empathy and not to be judgemental.

This means helping them understand how other people feel and encouraging them to put themselves in others' shoes. This can be done through simple things like hands-on activities like volunteering or doing acts of kindness for others. When children understand how their actions affect others, they're more likely to act with respect that will last a lifetime.

We are creatures of habit, so it's understandable that any changes or improvements in your family will take time, so be open, positive and patient and enjoy the journey.

Parenting is a hard but it's also very rewarding.

Sometimes it's amazing how much we don't know about our children. I remember attending a parents' evening at my children's school and we were asked to complete a quiz with a series of 20 questions aptly named "How well do you know your child?".

I, along with most parents attending that night, got a rude awakening, as most of us rated very poorly and I certainly was embarrassed by how little I really knew about my boys. Here are just some random questions (modify them for younger children) that could be great conversation starters.

1. What do they think are their greatest strengths?
2. What is their favourite subject at school?
3. What are they passionate about?
4. What do they have challenges with?
5. When was the last time you had an in-depth conversation with them?

Action Steps

List one item you will implement this week and one to schedule for the next.

- Tell your children that you appreciate them.
- When was the last time you said "thank you" to your children?
- Find ten things to be grateful for with your children.

Make two-way conversations a habit. Spend a few more minutes every night talking about anything, as your tiny humans become comfortable and at ease with you, you can learn more in-depth information and fill in the blanks.

Chapter 5

You're Already an Influencer....

But you will have competition so what can you improve?

As a parent, you will already have unique learnt behaviours and challenges, but a few golden rules will remain  love, involvement, learning, trust, open communication, and tailoring your approach to each of your tiny human's needs.

Parenting is like art – no one's perfect, but if you're guiding your children with love, you're on the right track.

And talking of the right track, I put to you that we do need to set clear boundaries for children of all ages – yep, even your teenagers. **Think of the boundaries as more like guardrails on a curvy road.**

They will keep your children safe and on track. Without them, things can get pretty wild, scary and unpredictable. And don't forget, a sprinkle of humour and a light-hearted touch can make this parenting journey a whole lot more enjoyable.

And lastly, before we go down the child development rabbit hole, I want to ask parents to consider right now, do you accept your children for who they are right now, or are you hoping to change them into being what you want them to be?

> I remember hearing this fantastic insight:
>
> It was about how, in fact, parenting is no different than being a shepherd. We offer our lambs (tiny humans) love, security and protection in the early years (well about 20 years actually) but ultimately, they are going to grow up to be their own individual creatures with their own journey in life.
>
>
>
> We do not own them, only guide them and hopefully equip them with the skills to handle the wolves (or sharks) out there and live a long prosperous life.
>
> Once we accept that this is our role, parenting becomes a lot more fun, easy and relaxed.

The imprint period

The "imprint period" in child development typically refers to the critical period from birth to around 7 years of age when children are super receptive to learning.

This is when they absorb stuff like language, culture, and social norms. It's a bit like their brain being a sponge, soaking it all up.

During this time, they're forming the foundation for their future cognitive, emotional, and social development. There's no doubt, this can be highly concerning for parents, so what if I tell you:

This can all be achieved effortlessly if parents can remember three simple words:

FUN - LAUGHTER - PLAY.

If you can incorporate this into your daily interaction with your tiny humans, you'll nail it.

Language acquisition

Children are language ninjas during the imprint period. Their brains slurp up sounds, words, and grammar like a smoothie. So, if they're in a linguistically rich environment, it sets them up for language success later on. Multilingual children have a breeze of a time picking up languages during this phase.

Social and emotional development

This is when children learn to become social butterflies. They figure out how to interact, develop empathy, and create bonds with caregivers. The quality of these early relationships is like a recipe for their emotional well-being down the road.

Cognitive development

This is when children level up their thinking game. They start building memory, problem-solving skills, and attention span. They're basically little explorers, learning to navigate their world and setting the stage for future smarts and school success.

Cultural and environmental awareness

Your tiny humans will start noticing the world around them. They pick up family traditions, community values, and their own cultural identity. It's like the foundation for their worldview.

Motor skills

Little ones are also busy bees developing their motor skills. They learn to walk, run, jump, and handle stuff. It's all part of becoming physically independent.

Sensory development

The five senses are in full action during this phase – sight, hearing, touch, taste, and smell. These experiences are like their tour guides to the world.

Early education and learning

The imprint period is a VIP time for early education. High-quality early learning experiences can have a long-lasting impact on a child's brainpower and social skills. So, if your tiny humans are curious, feed that curiosity.

The imprint period is like their super-learning phase, but that doesn't mean the learning stops at age seven. It just means their brain becomes a bit less bendy, and learning might need a bit more elbow grease.

Now, it's up to parents, caregivers, and educators to create the right environment during the imprint period. They need a safe, nurturing, and stimulating setting to help children grow and thrive.

In a nutshell, the imprint period from birth to seven years is when children are like sponges, soaking up life's lessons. It's the time for language, social and emotional skills, cognitive growth, and forming cultural awareness. Nurturing this phase leaves a lifelong impact on a child's development and well-being.

A quick overview of the other developmental stages

Remember - same rules apply: FUN - LAUGHTER - PLAY for your tiny humans.

Middle Childhood (7-12 years): This stage is all about logic, complex social skills, and building a sense of self. Children hit school and start exploring their interests.

Adolescence (13-19 years): Puberty, deeper thinking, independence, and identity exploration are the stars of this show. Parents, brace yourselves for a whirlwind of change.

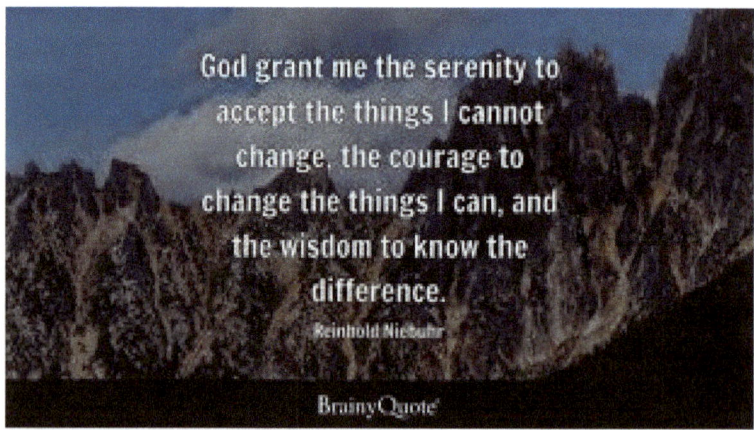

Now just repeat after me, the famous words by Reinhold Niebuhr

Action Steps

List one area of influence you will implement into the family this week and one to schedule for the next.

1. Are you doing too much for your tiny humans?
2. Name a challenge you can help them think of a solution.
3. Are you robbing them of their childhood?
4. Do your children have Chill out time?
5. How can you bring more Fun-Laughter-Play into your realm?
6. Try 3 new ideas or things to try this week.

Chapter 6

Is Your Parenting Style A Match?

Finding your unique balance

It is pointless trying to share with you the novelty of the many new parenting titles and themes our social platforms and media have invented (my favourite is the lawn mower parent).

As with any titles, I find them all a bit cliché, however in the realm of psychological research, four primary parenting styles have been extensively recognised. These styles are characterised by different combinations of parental responsive and demands. I will provide a very brief overview of these four primary parenting styles.

Authoritarian Parenting

Strict, controlling, demanding, disciplined, unresponsive, rule-focused, rigid, high-expectation, uncompromising, directive.

High demands - Authoritarian parents are known for their high expectations, setting numerous rules and standards for their children.

Low responsive - They may be less responsive to their child's emotional needs and may not exhibit much nurturing or affection.

Communication style - Authoritarian parents tend to communicate with a strict, controlling, and directive approach.

Impact on children - Children raised by authoritarian parents might excel academically and in their chosen activities. However, they can face challenges with independence, creativity, and may experience elevated levels of stress and anxiety.

Authoritative Parenting

Supportive, responsive, nurturing, structured, encouraging, balanced, communicative, consistent, understanding, empowering, as both crave power and control.

High demands - Authoritative parents have clear rules and expectations, but they are also flexible and open to adapting them based on their child's developmental stage and needs.

High responsive - They are emotionally supportive, nurturing, and responsive to their child's emotional needs.

Communication style - Authoritative parents employ a balanced and open communication style, involving their children in discussions and explanations.

Impact on children - Children raised by authoritative parents tend to be self-disciplined, socially competent, and have higher self-esteem. They perform well academically and maintain good emotional well-being.

Permissive (or permission) parenting

Lenient, indulgent, nurturing, non-directive, accommodating, low-discipline, friend-like, tolerant, relaxed, few-rules.

Low demands - Permissive parents have few rules and tend to be lenient. They are more likely to give in to their child's desires.

High responsive - They are nurturing and emotionally supportive, often prioritising the parent-child relationship over discipline.

Communication style - Permissive parents often use a non-directive approach and seek to avoid confrontations.

Impact on children - Children raised by permissive parents may have high self-esteem and feel loved. However, they can struggle with self-discipline, respecting authority, and following rules. Adapting to environments with clear boundaries might also pose challenges.

---

*Permissive In Extreme - Uninvolved (or neglectful) parenting

Impact on children- Children raised by uninvolved parents may experience neglect, have low self-esteem, and face emotional and behavioural problems. They may also struggle with attachment and social relationships.

*I am including this paragraph as there is an unacceptable level of child abuse and neglect happening in our very fabric of our society.

With the implementation of new laws, many western countries now has a responsibility to mandatory reporting, if we suspect a child is at risk of harm or have reasonable grounds for suspicion of physical, sexual, or emotional abuse, or neglect. Please check your legislation.

It's essential to recognise that most parents exhibit a blend of these parenting styles, which may evolve over time based on the child's age and developmental needs.

The authoritative parenting style is generally considered the most balanced and effective, combining clear rules and expectations with emotional support and open communication. However, effective parenting often involves adapting one's approach to the specific needs and temperament of the child.

Parents here focus on teaching their children, at any age, how to solve problems by contemplating and discussing alternative choices. There is clear involvement of parents, and children are given certain expectations about what is appropriate and what is not.

But it isn't a one-size-fits-all approach

Parenting is not about adhering strictly to a particular style. Don't try to put yourself into a box. **As your child's first and most influential teacher, remember that it's not about being a perfect parent but about being a guiding light.**

Every child is unique, and the journey of parenthood is about adapting to their evolving needs and celebrating their individuality. In this extraordinary adventure of parenthood, sprinkle in some childlike humour and lightheartedness.

What truly matters is the love, support and guidance you provide, creating a strong foundation and trust for their future.

There is no-one on this planet better equipped to understand and care for your "tiny human", so my advice is to test, track, laugh, love and apologise when you get it wrong.

The mere fact that you're reading this book shows you are committed and making time for yourself to get better for your children. I would not ask any more of you.

Congratulations, your child is lucky to have you; and if you get it wrong like I did often, understand you will learn from it.

So perhaps both parents need to give thought and discuss together: "What do you want most for your child?" Close your eyes and pretend you are a time-traveler, able to see ten or twenty years into the future. What do you want to see? Your child as an adult, healthy, happy, wise, compassionate? A great leader, an engaged parent, well-liked, successful, etc, etc, etc.

You decide. Now work backwards and think of how to provide these skills for your children. Perhaps you may just come to the realisation that "you should not be sweating the small stuff" (and it's all small stuff).

So is your parenting style matching your child's type/personality/traits (and needs)?

Understanding your parenting style is helpful but it is not enough, you need to also fully understand your tiny human's type/personality traits, only then you can put together a scientifically formatted plan for you to utilise.

Recent research on child personality offers us fresh insights into how your tiny humans develop their unique personalities and characteristic and how the correct parenting styles can successfully influence this process.

However, I first came across this concept, over 20 years ago in a book written by Dr Phil McGraw called Family First. It is a great book, and I certainly recommend you picking up a copy form the local library, it is a little dated and no longer in print. However, I have listed some similar questions to determine your child's primary style as well.

Whilst I do not believe in labelling or pigeon-holing our amazing Tiny Humans, I have also gone on to study personality traits and love language for children and found it proved me with invaluable insights.

Supporting Personality Growth in Different Ways

Researchers also point out that these traits aren't set in stone; our tiny humans' personalities can shift as they grow. For example, children who tend toward impulsiveness and big emotions may become more even keeled and dependable as they mature, if they have positive role models and consistent guidance

Understanding your child's personality can help you create a nurturing approach that matches their needs, supporting them in becoming confident, resilient, and emotionally balanced as they grow.

Key Personality Types or Characteristics in Children

Resilients (Cooperatives)

These are children who typically adapt well to new situations and tend to be emotionally stable.

For instance, if you make it a point to talk with your child about their day or emotions calmly, you're likely helping them build resilience. **A resilient child might handle a bad grade or a conflict with a friend without getting overly stressed.**

How does your child react to setbacks or failures?

Do they give up easily, or try again with different strategies?

Do they bounce back relatively quickly?

When faced with a challenge, does your child seek help or try to solve it independently?

Do they ask for help readily, or do they persevere on their own?

Do they view challenges as opportunities or threats?

How does your child handle changes in routine or unexpected events?

Do they become anxious or agitated, or adapt with flexibility?

Do they express frustration or find ways to cope with the change?

Over-controllers (passive)

Over-controllers are children who are highly self-disciplined but might struggle with anxiety or perfectionism. They may not be as outgoing and tend to be more cautious in social settings.

For instance, if your child is often nervous about making mistakes, you might help by encouraging them to take safe risks or reassuring them that it's okay to try again.

How does your child handle making mistakes?

Do they become very self-critical or upset?

Can they accept mistakes as part of learning?

Do they need to do things perfectly, or more relaxed about mistakes?

How do they react to situations that are not predictable or structured?

Do they try to impose order, or can they tolerate uncertainty?

Do they prefer routines or are they comfortable with spontaneity?

How do they express their emotions, ie anger or sadness?

Do they tend to internalise their feelings, or can they express them in healthy ways?

Do they worry about losing control of their emotions, or do they feel comfortable with emotional expression?

> **Under-controllers** (Rebellious)
>
> **These children are often more impulsive, have big emotions, and may struggle with rules or structure.** Research suggests that inconsistent discipline, like shifting between being overly strict and lenient, can contribute to out of control or unacceptable behaviour.
>
> For example, if a child frequently acts out in school or at home, creating a steady and predictable environment with clear boundaries, may help them feel more secure and gradually develop self-control.
>
> How does your child handle impulses or urges?
>
> Do they act without thinking, or do they consider the consequences?
>
> Do they have difficulty following rules, instructions or limits?
>
> Are defiant or easily frustrated, or can they accept boundaries?
>
> Do they struggle with self-regulation, or can they manage their behaviour effectively?
>
> How does your child approach tasks or responsibilities?
>
> Do they struggle with organisation, or can they complete tasks effectively?
>
> Do they tend to be easily distracted or have difficulty focusing, or can they sustain attention?

While each style reflects different approaches to setting boundaries, discipline, and support. The reason to look into your child's type is to for you to have confidence on the best way to interact with your child when different situations arise.

You become the adapter. And yes, if you have a few children, you have some homework to do, as I guarantee your love-able little tiny humans will fall into predominately different categories so it will be trial and error to work out what works and what doesn't.

Here's some "real world" suggestions

Authoritarian Parenting

Under Controller (Rebellious) children

You may experience power struggles and managing this child is extremely frustrating and confrontational as you both trying to dominate situations. Too many rules generally frustrate these children.

Tip - Generally move towards more of an authoritative approach. Avoid angry exchanges, listen more, be calm, compromise, stay patient and persist.

If your child has **Resilience (Cooperative)**

Expects some conflict as they like to be involved in family decision making or problem solving. They often like to be given responsibly which authoritarian parents are often reluctant to give.

Tip - Move towards the Authoritative Parents model, giving your child more decision-making responsibility, increase your involvement and encourage your child more often giving a more supportive and nurturing atmosphere.

Over controller, (passive)

Together you are a good fit, as your child need's structure and told what to do. They respond to your parenting style by using checklist and schedules this helps this child who are not normally self-starters.

Authoritative Parenting

If your child is an Under-controller (Rebellious)

Expect to have some trouble communicating as they do not seem to want to listen or share or give power away. They want it all.

Tips - This apparent selfishness can be frustrating for you however never overreact.

Let your child disagree with you on a topic however explain your point of view in a calm manner.

Let your child lead some family activities or events and include them in establishing ruses with appropriate behaviour and consequences.

If your child is **Resilience (Cooperative)**

Your relationship is already based on teamwork and is usually a good fit for success and interaction are generally positive. There is a peaceful co-existence here because you already relate well and accept each other.

Because parents often expect their **Over-controller (passive) children t**o enter eagerly into team activities, they can become frustrated as a passive child is often very reluctant to get involved, they may be shy or timid.

Tips - As a parent understanding this, you need to provide opportunities to expand their skills but in their own time.

Move towards a more Authoritarian style in order to provide structure and predictable schedule to allow the child to feel secure, be adaptable and flexible and patient.

Permissive Parenting

If your child is Under-controller (Rebellious)

The relationship works well because both you and your child are sympathetic towards each other. You both take an interest in what each other are doing.

Tip - Generally a parent is strong on support but may be weak on control. So if your child is cooperative, a permissive parent should learn how to place firm limits on any unacceptable behaviours.

If your child is Resilience (Cooperative)

This relationship is a good match but will have tensions emerge as often a permissive style may offer too much decision-making authority to this child.

A child could feel overwhelmed, disconnect and the communications between each could be poor.

Tip - Develop more two-way conversations, listening and being more active in problem solving and design making. Encourage your child to speak for themselves an express their feelings. Engage and work together on mutual program and activities.

If your child is an Over-controller (Passive)

This is not the ideal situation as the characteristics a passive child needs stimulation and direction from you.

Tips - Move to a more authoritarian style of parent for your child they need clear structure and boundaries to feel motivated.

Give more of yourself in terms of providing challenges and do more hands-on instruction for activities.

You become the adapter.

And yes, if you have a few children, you have some homework to do, as I guarantee your love-able little, tiny humans will fall into different categories which means you have to learn how to adapt **to avoid clashes and become a bit of a problems solver.**

But it will be trial and error to determine what works and what doesn't.

While each style reflects different approaches to setting boundaries, discipline, and support. The reason to investigate your child's type is for you to have confidence on the best way to interact with your child and when different situations arise.

Another parental tool worth utilising

The "Five Love Languages" was developed by Dr. Gary Chapman This framework identifies five primary ways in which people give and receive love. These love languages help individuals understand how they and their loved ones prefer to express and receive affection.

Understanding and responding to these love languages can strengthen relationships, including those between parents and their children.

- Words of affirmation.
- Acts of service
- Receiving gifts
- Quality time
- Physical touch

For Parents of very small children, I encourage all of the love languages be utilised but as children develop into tweens or teenagers,

astute parents will be able to identify their child's primary love language by observing their preferences and reactions.

It's important to note that children may still have a combination of love languages.

Action Steps

1. List one item you will implement this week and one to schedule for the next.

2. First establish what is your predominant parenting style, how has this been working for you?

3. Reflect on your children's primary characteristics. Utilise the questions provided in the last chapter.

4. Now re-read the combinations. List your thoughts in your journal.

5. Se a time for a discussion with your partner or significant other? (Put this under the micro-scope, discuss your thoughts.)

6. Allow me to suggest that you both keep a journal handy and together just jot down notes, insights or observations to different scenarios.

7. Identify one area you feel you can change?

"Being a parent is not about perfection,

it's about progress."

Chapter 7

Discover The SleepTalk® Solution.

The greatest gift, you will ever give your children.

Parenting can be like riding a rollercoaster in the dark. You never quite know what's coming next, and sometimes you scream, sometimes you laugh, and sometimes you just close your eyes and hope for the best.

In the midst of all this chaos, let's take a laid-back, slightly humorous look at what children truly need to thrive.

I am excited to say that in the following two chapters you are going to discover one of the simplest and easiest ways for your children to thrive. I believe it is one of the best kept parental secrets in the world, yet it has been around for more than 50 years.

It is called the SleepTalk® Process, and I want to ensure you gain a general understanding of the power of this simple process and how it can transform your children's attitudes and beliefs and offer your children a feeling of safety, resilience and unconditional love.

As a fully accredited SleepTalk® professional, nothing gives me more pride than to include details of the SleepTalk® process into this chapter. I do not believe there is a better opportunity for parents to utilise this process; whether you have terrible twos or tedious teens, you can start to make a difference with this process today.

Imagine creating a happy and positive world for both you and your family. Remember, the success of this SleepTalk® process is entirely dependent on you.

Children and families grappling with a spectrum of issues, including bedwetting, tantrums, trauma, stress, sibling rivalry and separation anxiety, have all demonstrated favourable responses to the SleepTalk® process. This includes children facing physical, emotional, or intellectual challenges.

The SleepTalk® process unfolds as a three-phase protocol in which parents deliver a sequence of affirmations to their slumbering child each night. These "statements," are the product of a husband-and-wife team, the Goldings both hypnotherapists who were struggling with their daughters' challenges. Five decades later, the SleepTalk Process, has continue to offer families all over the globe exceptionally beneficial in the cultivation of a positive self-image, the development of robust, constructive core beliefs, and the nurturing of a profound sense of unconditional love.

In the next chapter, I am going to share with you Phase One of the world-renowned Parental Program. For further assistance with more major childhood challenges, I will provide contact details to our fully qualified SleepTalk® professionals.

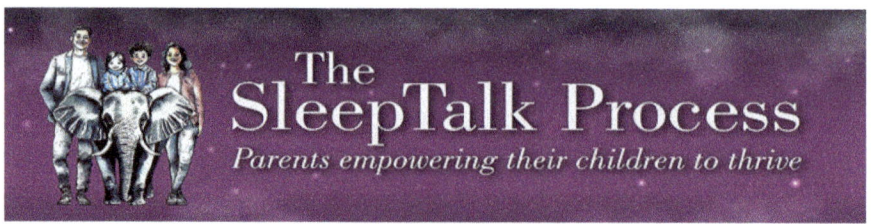

The SleepTalk® Process has been called the "Gift of a Lifetime"

The greatest gift you can give your children is the gift of unconditional love. Yes, that's right. Unconditional love means you'll love them, NO MATTER WHAT, even when they decide to paint the living room with peanut butter, fill your petrol tank with water or create a modern art masterpiece on your freshly painted walls.

Unconditional love - imagine if your children felt unconditionally loved no matter what!

Often, I've noticed that a positive attitude in children is closely tied to feeling loved and loveable. Irrespective of their success or failures, it's vital that your children genuinely believe that you love them and that they are loveable. You might say, "Well, I already love my children, and they know it!"

Undoubtedly, you do, and you probably express it regularly. However, what many of us fail to realise is that unintentionally, we and others send mixed or negative messages to our children. These messages can seep into a child's subconscious and can erode their confidence and hinder their journey towards reaching their full potential and lasting happiness.

In the hustle and bustle of parenting, as we set rules and strive to encourage appropriate behaviour, we often use phrases that, on the surface, seem harmless.

For instance, we might playfully say, "You're such a little terror!" as we give our small child a hug. We understand the humour behind it, but a child's world is quite literal. Messages like these, when repeated frequently, become part of their reality.

This seemingly playful message can be interpreted in various ways by a tiny little human: "She wants me to be a terror? Does she like me or not? I get rewarded when I'm a terror. Yesterday, I got scolded for it, but today I got hugged." This can lead to confusion, doubt, and create disharmony.

Negative messages can easily seep into our relationships with our children, forming communication habits that are challenging to break. Phrases like, "You're so clumsy!" or "You'd forget your head if it wasn't screwed on!" and, "He's just like me - hopeless at math!" are examples of innocent expressions of parental frustration. When repeated, they can inflict significant damage on a child's self-image and, consequently, their future.

We, as parents, are not the sole bearers of such comments. Children receive these negative or mixed messages from others in their lives, including childcare staff, schoolteachers, relatives, and even friends. Schools can be a breeding ground for negative suggestions. Sometimes, a challenging environment or specific circumstances can exacerbate these childhood challenges. The impact of media, peers, and social media on our children can't be ignored either.

The damage our words can do to our children (Courtesy of JGouldings)

Vanessa Lewis, a therapist, points out the significant impact parents can have on their children through their words. The slip of a tongue or an unintentionally hurtful remark can leave a lasting emotional scar.

Moments of parental frustration, where words are flung without thought, can pierce a child's heart. So, it's crucial to realise that our words hold incredible power, whether we use them intentionally or inadvertently.

In those stressful moments when we're tired and cranky, it's easy to utter words we don't mean. We might find ourselves saying things like, "How can you be so silly?" or "When will you learn to think?". These words, though they may offer temporary relief for us, can lead to lasting damage to our child's self-esteem and the trust between us.

We must recognise the importance of controlling hurtful language. A parent's ability to manage their own anger and frustration plays a crucial role in teaching a child how to behave. No-one is a perfect parent, but learning from our mistakes, forgiving ourselves and moving forward is the way to go.

Things not to say to your children Here are some statements that experts agree are used often by parents and are most harmful:

- "Why can't you be more like...?" - Every child is unique and an individual.

- "Why don't you act your age?" - Many times, when we insist a child act their age, they are!

- "Must you always look like such a slob?" - Criticism only lays the groundwork for an unproductive power struggle. The key is to strike a balance.

- "You're the funny one/athletic one/pretty one." - Labels we give children can be problematic, confirming and, when negative, are also demeaning. A negative label can become a self-fulfilling prophecy.

- "How could you be so stupid?" - 'Stupid' is a loaded word that can be especially damaging to a child's self-esteem and confidence.

- "Sometimes I wish I'd never had kids." – A child hears, "You're worthless, I wish you weren't my kid. I don't want you". Terrible hurtful messages a child carries around, often unconsciously, into adulthood.

- "Leave me alone!" - An angry dismissal of a child can make them feel unloved and unwanted.

- "Shut up!" – Apart from being impolite, degrading, controlling and demeaning, children learn by example.

- "If you don't come with me now, I'll leave without you." – The threat of abandonment as a discipline tool is a destructive approach to take and pretty scary for a child. It reinforces a fear that young children already have – that a parent might disappear and never come back.

It is never too late to learn - never too late to change. We all make mistakes. We need to learn from them, forgive ourselves and move on. The following alternative approach to family communication and issues may help:

- Encouragement vs praise: Encourage consistent progressive effort to achieve their best.
- Choices and Consequences: Indicates personal responsibility and consequences of choices made.

- Rejecting child's behaviour rather than the child: Before the child goes to sleep at night, correct any negative comments so they feel appreciated and worthy rather than resented.

It's not always possible to dealing with issues before sleep

So what do we do if this situation occurs? How do we deal with issues correctly? If possible, deal with the issue before sleep - sit down on the side of the bed and perhaps say to them,

"Darling, when I yelled at you, I was upset. Well, I'm like you, sometimes when I'm upset I say things I don't mean, and I really didn't mean what I said. I don't know what I would do without you. I love you."

We can present an alternative explanation and the solution to their dilemma straight away. When they go to sleep the explanation and the memory of distress will be accepted as a complete unit, as an already resolved issue, not a problem. In fact, a deeper understanding of the situation may occur. They may think, "Hey, Mum loves me, everyone gets upset sometimes. We all say things we don't really mean. It's OK though, they love me."

Sometimes, we forget that it's never too late to learn and make amends. **The SleepTalk® process, gives parents a second chance** to help reshape their children's self-image, replacing negative beliefs with positive ones. Think of it as "Happiness Insurance". SleepTalk™ has the ability to correct that situation.

Kerre Burley

It is so simple, yet so powerful.

Parents can provide a positive influence on your children's future whilst they are asleep.

The SleepTalk® Process phase 1 works wonders, allowing parents to counteract any damaging statements. It empowers them to assist their children to feel happier, be more balanced, and secure, and it only takes a few minutes every night.

All children, regardless of their abilities, attitude towards life, or current environment, benefit from this life-changing process. Similarly, Phase 1 of the SleepTalk® Process requires no more than about 3-5 minutes a night over a set period of 8-12 weeks to achieve the desired results.

Always keep in mind, SleepTalk® is a non-intrusive, natural process and takes only a short time for parents or carers to deliver.

I only discovered the SleepTalk® Process after my first four boys had grown up, so I was lucky enough to start the process on my youngest son, Sean. At the time, Sean was a well-adjusted and happy-go-lucky six-year-old that didn't have a care in the world.

My reasoning was, I just wanted him to feel comfortable and secure with himself.

Six months after we started Sean on the process, my husband and I decided to change our lifestyle - we sold our businesses and went overseas and we took Sean with us.

We literally pulled him out of school, took him away from his friends, family and comfortable home life and found ourselves in an unknown country, with an unknown language and lots of strange new experiences, literally. **I believe due to SleepTalk®, not only did he cope, but he thrived in this environment.**

What was meant to be 3 months turned out to be several years overseas and Sean's ability to stay positive, make friends and overcome obstacles proved priceless. I certainly can attest his childhood, and adolescence has been far easier than any of his brothers, and as a parent I found the road to parental bliss.

To this day, even as Sean has become a young man, we have a very healthy relationship and bond. So I would encourage all parents, if nothing else, to take this life-changing process and start utilising it immediately.

Today I take pride in sharing this secret concept to parents and professionals from all over the world. **Let's face it, families and parents like yourself, around the world need SleepTalk® now more than ever.**

As Pablo Picasso once said,

"The meaning of life is to find your gift and the purpose of life is to give it away".

Chapter 8

Phase 1 - The Foundation Phase

But first - The 3 x CCCs to Success

Imagine a simple process, that yields 100% positive change results when parents are

- **Committed** - We require a 2 - 3 month commitment from parents to deliver the first phase of the process.
- **Consistent** - A parent repeats the process daily (if possible) once the children have gone to sleep for around 3 - 5 minutes.
- **Compliant** - Parents do not alter the following statements as the statement have been carefully crafted to be both effective and non-intrusive.

So before we dive in, rest assured the SleepTalk® process is a safe and effective process for all children.

For some children who have experienced severe trauma, experienced the following contra-indicators **or are under the guidance of a medical professional or specialist therapist,** we strongly recommend seeking medical clearance then reaching out to a fully accredited.

SleepTalk Professional for your own peace of mind.

Contraindications

- Diagnosed mental disorder - extreme neuroses or anxiety
- Emotional instability - extreme distress - past trauma - extreme behavioural issues
- Extreme emotional distress - traumatic experiences - obsessive-compulsive disorder (OCD)
- Generalised anxiety disorder (GAD) - post-traumatic stress disorder (PTSD)
- Pathological demand avoidance (PDA) – self-harm - suicidal tendencies.
- Psychological stress related to paralysis, blindness, or seizures
- Gender identity confusion - gender identity disorder

Otherwise, all parents can just persevere each night and gradually discover their children improvements in these areas.

Anger, Anxiety, Bedwetting, Behaviour issues,Bullying, Coordination, Concentration, Confidence, Disobedience, Eating Disorders, Emotional outbursts, , Poor Habits, Nail-biting, Nightmares Night Terrors, Panic attacks, Selective Mutism, Self-esteem , Separation anxiety, Sibling rivalry, Sleeping Issues, Social challenges,

Speech , Night Stress, Tantrums, Toileting Issues, & phobias

For more information please visit the website.

https://thesleeptalkprocess.com

The Foundation Statement

Step 1 - Wait 45 minutes after your children have fallen asleep.

Step 2 - Walk (don't creep) into their rooms and position yourself just above them (you do not need to touch teenagers, poor sleepers or highly anxious children, in these cases, you can do it from the doorway)

Step 3 - If your child is facing you, gently stroke their forehead or if facing away from you, gently stroke from the crown of the head to the back of the neck. Look for a slight movement (it is called transference) a snuggle or licking of the lips. When that happens, we stop touching and begin with the process.

If during the process, your child starts to rouse, just return them to sleep by repeating the words:

"Deep asleep... deep asleep... happy dreams... waking up bright and happy... Mummy loves you... Daddy loves you... we all love you... you are loveable... today is a happy day." (All you need to do is repeat the statements regardless of the response.)

Or if you are concerned that they have awakened fully, simply tell them that you are just checking on them and you love them and leave the room. Then try again the next day.

Step 4 - Begin in a normal loving voice, (do not whisper) but say very, very slowly.

(Say once)

Stay asleep, Stay asleep, Stay asleep.

(Although the words may feel strange to you, they will not be, to your tiny human.)

(**Repeat the following statement five times** - Adjust to how your child addresses you, I.e Dad, Rick)

Mum loves you, Dad loves you, your brothers & sisters love you, "WE" all love you - you are loveable, today is a happy day.

(Return your child to natural sleep by saying once, the following.)

Deep asleep, deep asleep, happy dreams, waking up bright & happy.

Mum loves you, Dad loves you, your brothers & sisters love you, "WE" all love you, you are loveable. Every day in every way "IT" gets better & better.

(Emphasis the words "IT" and "WE")

Action Steps

- Ensure you utilise and deliver the process correctly and consistently to ALL children individually every night.
- Set a daily reminder on the phone around 45 minutes after the children have gone to bed.
- Enjoy getting into the habit of delivering this life-changing process for around 8 to 12 weeks per phase.
- Make sure you keep a journal or note down the positive changes you start to notice.
- After 8 to 12 weeks, you are welcome to continue or if there is further improvements required needing the more advanced Phase 2 and Phase 3 of the process reach out to our [Fully Accredited SleepTalk Professional](https://thesleeptalkprocess.com/category/consultant/)s via our website for further support and guidance.

(https://thesleeptalkprocess.com/category/consultant/)

Chapter 9

Master Effective Communication.

Now that you have just been given an "Ace up your sleeve", this process will create positive change. What else can you do to discover parental bliss?

Sure, mastering effective communication with your children might sound daunting, but hey, I'm here to make it as breezy as a day at the beach. Let's dive into this chapter where we'll explore some tips for becoming masterful communicator with you children.

You might have a chatty toddler or a moody, burly teenager, but don't fret - we're going to tackle this with a smile as understanding communication is essential.

We've got a poem variation that captures the power of words, showing how words can leave a lasting impact.
Sticks and Stones may break my bones, but words can also hurt me,
Sticks and stones break only skin while words are ghosts that haunt me.
Pain from words has left its scar on mind and heart that tender,
Cuts and bruises now have healed, it's words that I remember.
ANON

When it comes to communication, let's heed Winston Churchill and never, never never, give up (on your children!).

According to Mum, every dialogue with her daughter was a drama!

Once upon a time, there was a little six-year-old girl named Sarah, who loved to argue with her parents about everything. Every time her parents would give her an instruction; she would argue and debate the merits of their request. Her frustrated parents tried everything to get her to listen, from reasoning to yelling to threats, but nothing seemed to work. It was exhausting.

Both parents were busy professionals and had full agendas and limited time.

One day, I encouraged her parents to try a new approach. They asked her to host a tea party, and they made time in their diary for the event. Both parents explained to Sarah that she could use it to talk on any topics she chose. Both parents listened attentively as their daughter played dress-up, opened up the conversation whilst pouring the tea and covered an array of subjects, giving her point of view.

Both parents remained engaged, present, and to their amazement, the time passed quickly and was most enjoyable. They came to realise that Sarah did have a very enquiring mind, and although she was stubborn, obstinate and resistant in many of their previous communications, given time to share her thoughts and reasoning, lots of her comments and feelings made sense.

When the tea party was over Sarah's parents thanked her for her time and told her they would like to organise more tea parties on a regular basis. Many of the previous challenges and stalemates were no longer an issue. Considering Sarah's point of view allowed them as a family to work through them. Future tea parties opened discussions around limiting time, compromises and options for solutions.

To their surprise, Sarah's demanding behaviour started to change, her parents were much softer in their approach and Sarah has become much more agreeable without further debate or opposition.

Sarah's parents made the commitment to weekly tea parties (quality time) with their daughter. Later, they admitted to me that they had never really listened to her before, nor given her reasons for their requests. Now they do both.

Both parents have very dominant personalities, so this simple tea party was a break through, It's evident they are much less demanding, and as a result, Sarah cooperates much more freely now.

Make Communications a Habit. Get good at communicating with your child whatever their age. Tech & covid has severely hampered out tiny humans' ability to communicate. So, it's up to parents to lead the way. If you err be bold enough to say sincerely,

I got very good at apologizing to my last son. Regrettably, it was not a skill I had with my first four boys. However, I do believe it is imperative for parents to leave their egos at the door when they have erred.

"I made a mistake, I didn't mean it, I do love you, it was your behaviour that annoyed me not you, I didn't mean those things I said today".

As a result, your child may not feel quite so guilty when they do the same thing or say something that they didn't mean. They may also come back to you and say, "

Hey, I'm sorry, I didn't mean it".

That's a rather lovely quality to give to your child, isn't it? The courage, the confidence, the self-esteem and the security to be able to say those things.

Communication is a two-way street.

Children need a safe space to openly express their thoughts and feelings, even if it's a 20-minute monologue on the intricate plot of a cartoon show. And don't forget, they appreciate when you share your thoughts and stories. It can be surprising how relatable you are.

Listening is key, especially when your child shares their ever-fascinating dinosaur facts during dinner, for the thousandth time. These moments are precious, and someday they'll move on to new topics like steam trains or superheroes.

Verbal communication is the most familiar, encompassing talking, shouting, whispering and everything in between. But have you considered nonverbal communication? This includes body language, facial expressions, and tone of voice. So, when your child says, "I'm fine" with crossed arms and a snippy tone, it's a safe bet they're not fine. Investigate further; there's more beneath the surface.

When you communicate with your children, active listening is vital.

It means giving them your full attention (that means full eye contact, parents, and LISTENING, not just waiting for them to finish so you can express your pearly words of wisdom opinion). When you speak to your children, try using "I" statements instead of "you" statements. Instead of saying, "You're not listening to me," say, "I feel like I'm not being heard." This minor change can have a significant impact on how your children perceive the message.

In my experience working with children for many years,

I've learned that children only retain about 8% of the words we say and forget 100% of our instructions within a week and that's normal.

Therefore, words alone aren't very effective in our teaching environment. **Our team worked really hard on emphasising animation, facial expressions, and body movements as our primary means of communication, and I encourage parents to do the same. If we must use words, ensure they're short, to the point, and filled with positive energy.**

You know, as parents, we have all made mistakes when communicating, especially to our children. We all need to learn from those mistakes, forgive ourselves, take the learning, leave the negative memory behind, and just move on. After all, it's about progress, not perfection.

Communication should be fun, even with teenagers who may often retort to open questions with one-word answers, i.e. "whatever". Create safe spaces, use humour and maintain a sense of humour in **your conversations. By making your message engaging and relevant and non-threatening**, it's still important to be observing their body language and reading the signs. Understand that they may be distracted, troubled or just not be in the mood?

Remember that building trust is key, it's not the end of the world to ask, **"I can see you don't feel like talking now, but can we catch up for a few minutes after dinner?"** or, **"I can see you haven't had a good day, how can I support you?"**.

Remember, parenting is about progress, not perfection. Remember, even the most stubborn of children will surprise you. It's all about listening, understanding and building trust to foster better communication.

As parents, we're used to being the ones in charge, but that doesn't mean we should always get our way. **As our children grow and develop, we do need to encourage them to negotiate and comfortably share with us their feelings, thoughts and ideas. Encourage your children to find compromises or solutions that work for both of you.**

It's much easier to start engaging in regular conversation with your children when they are younger, but the same principles can still apply to more resistant teenagers as well.

What if you can't get the children to engage?

This might mean setting a technology curfew in the evenings or creating a "no phones at the dinner table" rule. **"Conversations of change" are a great way of implementing new and clear boundaries in place.**

Often a conversation of change clearly identifies why this is important and offers older children an opportunity to have input into the new action.

Whilst I believe using persuasive language or influence on a teen is counter-productive, especially if communication has been ruptured.

I do believe every relationship is different and as caring parents we can plant seeds, make suggestions through open dialogue to get our message across.

Teenagers are good at getting up in a huff and leaving the room before any mutual solutions resolved. So I found my most successful meeting place was in the car before heading home (30 minutes away) from footy training.

I often would pre-frame the conversation coming, provide them with drinks and snacks and we would discuss the challenge before I would turn the car on and headed home. It was brilliant.

This means I had given thought to my topic and knew what I wanted to get across. **Speaking calmly, using simple words and phrases, and being patient when they don't understand your point of view right away. Then shutting up and letting them do the talking, if that means sitting in silence for 10 minutes, then so be it.**

Some Children Just Need Time!

We call them "period of time" learners and it is imperative that these children need time to think and weigh up their options before they can make up their minds, so a quick retort or answer will not come until they are ready.

There is nothing worse than hearing uneducated parents, teachers or educators trying to rush - or worse, ridicule - these children in front of their peers.

My eldest son Brent was a period thinker, and it was my greatest regret that it was many years before I came to realise this. As a business owner, I was always in a hurry, spoke too quickly and was often rushed when I was having discussions with him. (I still today make decisions quickly and rely on my gut, sometimes to my detriment.)

I would get so frustrated with the one-sided conversations with no response or solutions ever being achieved.

It was only when doing my NLP training when my son was a teenager, that it hit me like a sledgehammer where the breakdown in communications was coming from.

Think of the words, "Hurry up" parents use so many times every day. What does it really say to your tiny human? "I don't have time for you", "I have something more important than you" or "You're wasting my time"

Since realising my mistake, I now can prepare my son in advance and often pre-frame our up-and-coming chats, send emails prior to our catch up and list questions or issues I want to talk about.

This gives him plenty of time to be prepared. Even though my son is now a full-grown man, our communications are now so much more powerful and enjoyable.

I slow down and simply enjoy his company and his responses. Given time, he astounds me still to this day with his intellect and insights.

Some children also hate change, so sharing with them what is coming up (pre-framing) is an excellent skill for parents to learn and adapt.

Many parents with children on the spectrum can also utilise pre-framing to prepare children for what they might encounter, and by thinking ahead we can be better prepared to handle any possible challenges or unexpected changes.

Safe words, safe spaces and "Conversations of change" work well (on our children) and should go into the parent's utility belt.

Building rapport - creating a sense of trust and understanding

One way to build rapport with your children is through matching or mirroring, which is the matching of body language, tone of voice, and words.

This creates a sense of deep subconscious understanding and connection between you and your children, which can make it easier to communicate effectively.

However we also should take the time to get to know our children. If you have been utilising our end of chapter activities, you will have already discovered how to become more authentic with your tiny humans.

But we often forget the power of a simple smile!

> Again, I will refer to our "Giggles Swim Schools", we worked really hard on making our environment, services and our products as fun and non-threatening. Our swimming teachers were called "laughter leaders", and our lifeguards were called "play pals". **We hired a swim coach purely on her smile and fun attitude.**
>
> While many would like to argue that teaching children to swim or training swimmers is a serious business, **our team learnt that lightening up was the key and our greatest assets were our smiles and laughter.**
>
> I believe parenting is much the same, it's simple when you let go and don't take yourself too seriously. Pulling a goofy face, wearing a funny hat, even dancing a little jig can create priceless moments between you, your spouse and your tiny humans.

Don't take their hostilities and statements personally

This can be especially difficult when your children (or teenagers) are tired, hungry, angry or distracted, but the key is to make your message interesting and relevant for your tiny humans. This means using simple language, keeping your message short and sweet, with no more than three direct and easy-to-understand themes or instructions and using examples that your children can relate to.

I would like a dollar for every time I said to my second son, Luke who as a head strong teenager had a shocking temper and would fly into a rage with all sorts of negative statements directed at myself.

"Now I can see you are angry with me, Luke and when you are feeling ready to talk quietly about this, just let me know. In the meantime remember that I love you, I am sorry I have upset you and am here for you"

This statement literally took the wind out of his sails and this helped settle him down as he stomped out of the room muttering only to return a few hours later ready for our chat.

A mother and her teenage son were having a difficult time communicating as often were both angry with each other. The son always seemed to ignore her, and the mother was getting increasingly frustrated. One day, the mother decided to try something different. She wrote dozens of simple sticky notes with funny faces and stuck them all over the house.

When he arrived home, the son was surprised to find the notes everywhere he looked, including on his bedroom ceiling and even in the toilet bowl. He couldn't help but laugh. And just like that, the communication barrier was broken. He couldn't help but give his mum a big cuddle and open a dialogue about the toilet sticky.

From that day on, they made sure to always have a little bit of fun in their communications with each other.

Getting your tiny humans to follow instructions

This can be especially tricky when your tiny human is feeling stubborn, defiant or oppositional. But again, the key is to use simple language and to be patient. It's also important to break instructions down into smaller, more manageable steps (I say the magic number is three) and to use positive reinforcement to encourage your children to follow.

Remember to give your tiny human a valid reason. And "Because I said so" is not a valid reason.

My Late-Night Solution

As my teenage boys started to attend the local parties, as a single Mum I thought I had established a midnight curfew and had an understanding from them to leave the parties at midnight, so I could safely drive them home.

My boys were normally really good. So, imagine my disbelief as, repetitively, I found myself sitting outside of the party house sometimes till 1 or 2 am in the morning, freezing and waiting, waiting, waiting for them to come out to the car, weekend after weekend.

I still remember being so frustrated and annoyed at their inconsiderate attitude as I had to start work at 6am. Nothing seemed to work for weeks, until one night, I started thinking about what was important for teenage boys. And yes, I considered, teenage boys do not normally think through or consider consequences for their actions (as we all know, the world revolves only around them).

I sat down one night at the dinner table and had a very relaxed and calm conversation with both boys. I clearly and very calmly told the boys that whilst I was happy for them to continue to go to parties with their friends, however that in future, if they were not in the car by midnight, I would simply come into the party house and look for them (dressed in my bright pink dressing gown and fluffy slippers). I clearly stated that I was getting far too tired for my 6am starts.

They knew quite well, I was quite ok to do this, it was not an idle threat.

Well, you guessed it, the thought of their mum embarrassing them in front of their friends was just too much, and a very powerful motivator that allowed them to keep track of the time.

It worked a treat - they were never late to the car again. (Luckily for me using possible embarrassment and peer pressure worked to my advantage.)

Action Steps & Tips:

- Say daily "Thank you" and "I'm sorry – I made a mistake."
- Keep a diary/journal to analyse your feelings and responses to stressful occurrences in your parenting journey. This will help you discover your best outcomes to responses. Remember to Trail, Test and Note.
- Plan regular family dinners without devices to promote bonding and communication.
- Be available when they need to talk. Try to set up a regular weekly time in your diary.
- Schedule one-on-one time with each child every month. Make it a priority.

Strive to improve your communication, and you'll build stronger connections with your children. Communication is the key that unlocks the treasure of a nurturing, lasting parent-child relationships.

Chapter 10

Autonomy - The Parenting Pillar We Often Overlook.

In the midst of discussing masterful communication, let's not forget the vital concept of autonomy in parenting.

Autonomy means giving our children choices and letting them make decisions for themselves. When children feel in control of their lives, they experience respect and value. This can be achieved through everyday choices, such as letting them pick their outfits or choose dinner, or through more significant decisions like their choice of extracurricular activities. When children have a say, they tend to treat others with respect.

In this fast-paced world, raising respectful children isn't a walk in the park, but it's achievable and undoubtedly worthwhile. By leading through example, teaching empathy and empowering children with autonomy, you're equipping your little ones for a brighter future. Remember, it's not about perfection; it's about giving your best and enjoying the journey.

Here are some key points to consider.

Set boundaries, routines & frameworks. Creating a healthy home environment relies on setting clear rules and consequences and sticking to them. This approach reduces stress and fosters a more positive, peaceful home for everyone.

Involving your children. Encourage your children (depending on their age) to take ownership of setting these boundaries and consequences. Engage them in conversations and motivate them to contribute their ideas.

It's a life skill that will serve them well. The joy of parenting lies in witnessing your children evolve into the remarkable individuals you've always hoped they'd become.

Encouragement. (even if they want to be a stripper) Children harbour dreams and imaginations that can rival their wildest sock choices. Encourage them, even when their ambitions seem outlandish. It's worth remembering that creativity knows no bounds.

Independence. Give your children space to explore their independence, within reasonable limits. Teach them essential life skills, like making their bed or pouring cereal without triggering a breakfast catastrophe. However, keep those life jackets out of their reach if they decide to play pirates in the bathtub!

Gratitude (because the world needs more thank you notes). Teach your children to appreciate the small blessings in life. Cultivating gratitude helps them recognise the kindness that surrounds them, such as the neighbour who bakes extra cookies for them.

Adventure. Nurture a sense of curiosity and adventure. Take family trips, explore nature, and expand their horizons. Consider family documentaries for rainy days; they're a fantastic adventure for the mind.

Parents. It's perfectly okay to teach your children to admit fault or accept failure. Striving for perfection can lead to nothing but disappointment. Celebrate the effort instead. Allowing your children to fail is a means of encouraging them to be open, take responsibility, and strive for improvement.

Positive Examples

- When your child helps their sibling without being asked, they're showing empathy and respect.
- When your child apologises for their mistake and makes amends, they're demonstrating responsibility and respect.
- When your child calmly expresses their emotions and needs, they're learning effective communication and respect.

The concept of learned helplessness

It's easy for parents to become fixers of their children's problems. However, we must realise that constantly fighting their battles doesn't allow them to grow into effective problem solvers or overcome challenges on their own.

While on a walking track, I observed a father repeatedly pushing his young daughter on her bike up the small hills, only for her to coast down the other side, where she'd stop and then wait for him to catch up and push her up the next small incline.

While you could say it was a great bonding experience for dad and his daughter. This reminded me of the concept of learned helplessness and how it is not good for parents to encourage.

To me, it seemed the father missed an opportunity to teach his daughter self-reliance; by encouraging her to use her momentum and pedal up the next hill herself, she could be learning how to gain momentum overcome discomfort and pushing through to overcoming the next hill, achieving independence, self-reliance and succeeding on her own.

When our children become young adults and still are seeking you to fix everything, it might be a tough pill to swallow. But stepping back will be essential for their growth.

The joy of parenting is watching your children grow into the people you always hoped they would become.

In the words of Harold B Lee

"The most important work we will ever do is within the walls of our home."

Here is perhaps my biggest failing as a parent - the lesson that I had to learn.

Being a single parent for many years, I felt I had to be both Mum and Dad for my children. I would go and fight for my sons. I don't know how many times I stomped into their school, ready to right their injustices that they experienced at school, controlling and fixing things. Pulling up teachers, principals and anyone else that was messing with my children (I'm sure many of you, may be doing the same thing).

Now I understand that not only was this behaviour very embarrassing for my children with their teachers and peers, but it also robbed them of learning to solve their own problems and finding solutions to their school yard challenges. I did the same when one son continued on to uni.

Looking back now, I am quite embarrassed about my aggressive behaviour and attitude towards their teachers and staff. Of course, with age comes wisdom, and I realise now that there are always times for a parent to step in, but mostly, a wise parent knows when to step back.

My last son benefited enormously from my new-found wisdom. He would share with me many of his challenges and concerns about school, friends, peers and difficulties.

By generating the discussion and just asking him questions, he would come up with solutions and strategies on his own. I remember quite distinctly asking many times, "Would you like me to talk to your teacher?" and always respecting his answer, which was normally, "No thanks, Mum. I've got it".

Action Steps

What can you incorporate into your children's lives to help them be more autonomous over the next three weeks?

What can you teach them to do?

1

2

3.

Chapter 11

The Ever-changing Family Dynamic.

Parenting is an evolving journey, and in today's ever-changing landscape, it's crucial to adapt to the shifting dynamics of family units. Family structures have transformed significantly over the years, leading to adjustments in parenting dynamics. But even when exploring these changes and how they affect the way we raise our children, I will re-integrate all family circumstances are unique and you are in the perfect position to find solutions through trial and error and education.

Traditional nuclear family versus modern family structures

In the past, the nuclear family, comprised of two parents and their biological children, was the most common family structure.

Gender roles were often more rigid, with mothers predominantly responsible for childcare and fathers as the primary breadwinners.

Extended family members, like grandparents, aunts, and uncles played significant roles in supporting and raising children. Parenting responsibilities were well-defined, with less flexibility in roles and expectations.

Today, family structures and cultures are incredibly diverse, including single-parent families, stepfamilies, same-sex families, and many more. Gender roles have become more flexible, with fathers taking on more active roles in childcare, and mothers often juggling both work and family responsibilities.

Blended families, with stepparents and stepsiblings, require adjustments in parenting dynamics to accommodate multiple parental figures.

Changes in Parenting Dynamics

Shared parenting. Modern parenting emphasises a more equitable distribution of childcare and household responsibilities. Both parents often share the role of caregiver, leading to more balanced and fulfilling family lives however that doesn't always happen in real life.

Individualised parenting. Parents today have more access to information and resources, enabling them to tailor their parenting styles to their children's unique needs however it can be overwhelming. This individualised approach fosters greater autonomy and self-expression among children.

Diverse support systems. With different family structures, support networks have expanded beyond traditional extended families. Friends, support groups, and online communities will provide valuable sources of advice, empathy, and shared experiences.

Emphasis on Communication. Open and honest communication between parents and children has become central to modern parenting. Parents encourage children to express their feelings and ideas, fostering a more inclusive and empathetic family environment.

In summary, family units have evolved significantly over the years, leading to changes in parenting dynamics.

Today, parents are often more involved in their children's lives, with a greater emphasis on shared responsibilities, individualised parenting approaches, and an expanded support system.

However, life is much more chaotic. Communication and adaptability are key factors in navigating the complexities of modern family structures and ensuring the well-being of children.

Technology and online communities have allowed families to re-locate, connect and seek parenting advice from various sources, not just extended family members. However, the enormity of being a parents has never been greater.

Despite an over-whelming abundance of parental educators, well-meaning medical and therapeutic practitioners offering relief. Parents need to have confidence in their abilities. This is why parental education is so important.

I am hoping I have convinced you to lighten up as you do not have to be that drill sergeant. It's also important to be more childlike, goofy and silly too, and as we discussed in the last chapter, incorporating playtime into your parenting routine is a great way to bond with your children and show them that you're human too.

> *"Being a parent is an attitude, not a biological relation" -*
> *Robert A. Heinlein*

When I first became a single mum of my boisterous children, I thought I had to be both mother and father, often I would be very strict and harsh, making many unrealistic demands on them.

I used to yell so much at them from morning to noon that as I previously mentioned, eventually developed nodules in my throat and required surgery.

For the sake of my voice, I ultimately had to re-think my communication and found myself speaking to my children in a much softer, gentler manner and appeared calmer and so much more in control. What I discovered was revolutionary - all my children responded much more positively.

Raising tiny humans can be a challenging and stressful task, but it doesn't have to be!

Chapter 12

Parenting In the Digital Era.

Hey there, tech-savvy parents!

Welcome to the wild world of parenting in the digital era, where convincing your children to eat veggies is a cakewalk compared to prying smartphones from their hands.

As technology races ahead, I'm here to share some laid-back tips on navigating the digital landscape with your mini techies.

First off, allow me to upset you all right from the get-go. According to the latest research on screen-time recommendations, the amount of screen time that is considered safe and healthy suggests that our tiny humans under two should have absolutely no screen time at all.

And children between two and five years should see less than an hour a day. Of course, I know this will upset all those parents who use the screens to entertain their toddlers, but you do have to ask, is this really good for your baby?

Over the next few years, I imagine there is going to be a lot more research reach the main stream, so please ensure you stay abreast of what comes out, that way you are not sticking your head in the sand.

According to the latest research at the time of writing this chapter, in Australia, 94% of children by the age of 4 are on the internet and 95% are online from the age of 2 to 17 years of age.

Connect digitally, connect emotionally

The digital age is a tricky beast, but believe it or not, it's also a chance to bond with your children.

If your children are older, before setting boundaries, work together on a media plan. You ask the question then listen. What does your child feel is appropriate? What's should be the norm in your household? (Don't do just what everybody else is doing)

Explain the "why"s – what's in it for them?

Yes, there is no doubt, the internet has opportunities that far exceed anything that was around in the last generation. We can learn, play and socialise in seconds.

However, I believe it is a parent's responsibility to ensure their children are not at risk.

This means,

- Keep abreast of the research
- Be involved - learn and explore the digital world together.
- Stay close by - check in and supervise regularly.
- Experience and learn something "new" together online, i.e. new game or app or videos.

Our parents had it easy, they only had to worry about telling us about "the birds and the bees". In this day and age, this is another discussion we have to have to keep our tiny humans safe. **Our online safety discussion.**

An open, rational discussion about online games and addictions, the risk of predators, online security, hidden expenses and charges. We need to install in our children a sensible approach to social media usage, limited screen time and how they can enjoy a good balance of positive and fun technology usage and entertainment.

Set guidelines and keep an eye on their online adventures, purchases and apps, discuss options about responsible digital use and consequences if boundaries get stretched. Then put "IT" (your media plan) in writing - clearly set it out in simple, easy-to-understand language. Of course, if your children are very small, this then becomes a discussion with your partner.

Kerre Burley

> My non-negotiable suggestions are,
>
> - No phones, devices and screens in the bedroom after 10pm
> - No phones or devices at meal times or at the table (and that includes parents)
> - No phones or devices during family discussion / events
> - Limit of six hours over the weekends

Don't forget, all tiny humans require a "why", so do some research and quote some of the statistics out there that justify limited use. Lyn Maclean is Australia's foremost consumer educator on electromagnetic radiation.

She has written an amazing book called **Wireless-Wise Families: What Every Parent Needs to Know About Wireless Technologies**. She guides parents through this maze and shows clearly, in simple practical terms, what you need to know to live wisely in our ever more connected world.

Tech-savvy parent alert

Parents, you're crucial too! Embrace your unique perspective, and don't shy away from parenting duties. Your support and guidance are invaluable in this digital parenting journey.

Here's a tip: having challenges with getting children off their devices? Turn off your modem, change the password and wait in the room for the children to come.

This is a great time for a family "conversation of change" or even a "regular meeting or get-together regarding solutions".

But remember these are not opportunities for parents to lecture or vent so the more input our tiny humans have into some of our concerns the better. Keep it short and simple and focus on one or two points. My catch cry: "a short meeting is a good meeting".

Monitoring online adventures

With social media bullying and harassment on the rise, keep tabs on what your children are up to online. Ensure they're not wandering into unsuitable content or chatting with strangers. It's the 21st-century version of keeping an eye on the neighbourhood.

Digital Literacy 101

Tech is here to stay, so teach your children the ropes. Guide them on responsible and ethical use, throw in a lesson on online privacy, and sprinkle some cybersecurity knowledge. It's like giving them a superhero cape for the digital world.

Balance, baby!

Tech is cool, but so is playing sports, reading a good book, or just soaking up the great outdoors.

Encourage your children to embrace non-digital fun, striking the perfect tech-life balance.

If we are not careful, technology can erode communication in the family. Do not let this happen.

When all else fails, volcano time

Sometimes, you just need to make a dramatic exit. If all else fails, consider ceremoniously tossing their devices into the nearest volcano. Okay, maybe not literally, but you get the idea.

Finding a healthy home balance

Creating a healthy home environment in this digital age is crucial. Start with setting clear boundaries and having those "conversations of change" with your children. Explain the "why", involve them in solutions, and unleash their problem-solving skills.

Lead by example

Practise what you preach. If devices are off-limits at certain times, resist the urge to sneak a peek. Be the tech-savvy role model your children need.

Device-free activities

Ditch the screens and bond as a family. Board games, nature walks or cooking together – choose activities that disconnect your children from technology.

Seek professional EMF guidance

If you're EMF-worried, consider professional testing services. They can identify potential exposure sources and help you navigate the world of EMFs.

Remember, it's not just about tech boundaries; it's about creating a thriving, balanced home. So, set those rules, have those chats, and let the digital parenting adventure begin!

Action Steps

List 5 things you can do do today to make a safer home?

1.

2.

3.

4.

5.

The Joys of Parenting.

Oh, the joys of parenting,

It's a wild and wonderful ride,

With laughter and tears and tantrums and cheers,

It's a journey that will never be denied.

From the moment they're born,

Till the day they're grown,

We'll be by their side,

Guiding them as they've flown.

We'll teach them to walk,

And talk, and tie their shoe,

We'll kiss away their tears,

And wipe away their goo.

We'll watch them grow,

And learn, and play,

And we'll do it all over again,

Every single day.

So here's to the joys of parenting,

The ups and the downs,

We'll be there through it all,

With love and with crown

Further Recommended Reading.

Now relax - I know some are quite dated but don't hold that against my suggestions. Remember Bruce's words

"Absorb what is useful, discard what is not, and add what is essentially your own."

Not a reader - Don't use this as an excuse. Head to your local library and see if you can get the audio versions.

Title	Author
"Hold Onto Your Children: Why Parents Need To Matter More Than Peers"	Dr Gabor Mate/Gordon Neufeld
"The Five Love Languages of Children" & "Teenager	Gary Chapman
Babies, Toddler Taming, Beyond Toddlerdom	Dr Christopher Green
Family First	Dr Phil McGraw
The Secret to Happy Children, Raising Boys	Steve Biddulp
Raising Girls	Gisela Preuschoff
"The Brain That Changes Itself"	Normal Doidge
Psychologist the destructive effects of entitlement and praise	Dr Stephen Groszen
The Explosive Child	Ross Green
Parent Effectiveness Training	Dr Thomas Gordon
The Parenting Revolution	Maggie Dent
Good Inside	Dr Becky Kennedy

Final Word From The Author.

I would like to acknowledge all the guiding angels I have had in my life over the last 40 years of parenting.

As an avid reader with a thirst for coping skills for my own tribe, there have been so many its impossible to list starting from Dr Spock, Dr Christopher Green, Stephen Biddulp to modern day family experts like Dr Phil Mcgraw, Becky Kennedy and Justin Coleman, **so many others imparting little words of wisdom through the years, sharing with me that we are not alone and capable of more than we know.**

To the Golding's for creating the amazing SleepTalk® Process, I thank you, the positive ripple effects still happening half a century later from your creation is truly amazing.

To each and everyone, thank you, I am hoping in some small way this book assists you to find your way in this amazing journey. And please pay it forward to others.

I remember son's number 3 Dale, who was about 10 years of age, randomly asking me quite seriously whilst I was in the kitchen peeling potatoes, **"Mum, what is the meaning of life?"**

Now, I had learnt that random questions from curious, inquisitive children are just a normal part of life for parents. But on this occasion, the answer just came out instantaneously. I replied quite easily, **"Why you are, my son!"**

Now many years later, my boys have all left home, scattered around the world and have children of their own. Some stay in touch regularly, some not so much. Yet, when I think about it, I still marvel at the enormity of my answer all those years ago. I still sometimes ponder, where did that reply actually come from?

Yet, it is still as relevant today as it was back then.

I feel being a mother was, and still is, the most important thing I have ever done. And yes, my parenting duties have had their moments, but I would not have missed it for the world.

So, there you have it, sharing information with you, my second calling. Let's wrap it up in one quick final sentence from Gretchen Rubin.

Parenting - the days are long, but the years are short.

Go forth my friends and enjoy each and everyone of them.

Kerre Burley

www.ingramcontent.com/pod-product-compliance
Lightning Source LLC
Chambersburg PA
CBHW042319090526
44583CB00025BA/3183